GRACE TO DO
IT WITH DIGNITY

GRACE TO DO IT WITH DIGNITY

'C'JPB

Copyright © 2021 by 'C'JPB.

All rights reserved. No part of this book may be reproduced in any form or by any electronic or mechanical means, including information storage and retrieval systems, without permission in writing from the publisher, except by reviewers, who may quote brief passages in a review.

ISBN: 978-1-63821-647-6 (Paperback Edition)
ISBN: 978-1-63821-648-3 (Hardcover Edition)
ISBN: 978-1-63821-646-9 (E-book Edition)

Scripture taken from the Holy Bible, King James Version (Authorized Version). First published in 1611. Quoted from the KJV Classic Reference Bible, Copyright © 1983 by The Zondervan Corporation.

Book Ordering Information

Phone Number: 315 288-7939 ext. 1000 or 347-901-4920
Email: info@globalsummithouse.com
Global Summit House
www.globalsummithouse.com

Printed in the United State of America

Contents

Introduction vii
Success ix
Poem xi

Chapter 1   Life's Intruders 1
Chapter 2   The Challenges of Life/Job 9
Chapter 3   The Attacks of the Enemy 17
Chapter 4   Motives Defined 27
Chapter 5   Life 33
Chapter 6   Homeless 45
Chapter 7   Perseverance 52
Chapter 8   The Training 61
Chapter 9   The Victory 64
Chapter 10 Endurance 72
Chapter 11 A New Ministry 77
Chapter 12 Some Important How-To's: 79

Love is What Counts 86
Love that Counts 87
Love That Really Counts: 89
Grace To Do It With Dignity 91
Positive Words To Live By: 100
A Word of Thanks… 103
Biography 107

Introduction

As I write this book, I pray it will help you to become free and delivered from those bondages which impede your progress to go forward.

Success is waiting for you. In fact, success is looking for you. Success is following you right now. Success is at your door knocking for you to let success in. Open the door of your heart, and embrace success with kindness and love, and success will move you into other successful venues. It will be so unreal at a point you may think that it is a dream, but it will be reality setting in for the stage has already been set. God set it a long time ago. It was just waiting for you to embrace your future, destiny, blessing, and prosperity.

These experiences at a point I thought were a dream, and some were nightmares, but really and truly, it was reality setting in to shift me into higher heights and deeper depths with Christ. It was a storm with many storms that I had to embrace to go to the other side of all that God had and has for me. As you read this book, God will unfold the greatness that He has placed in you that has been smothered by so many things that the enemy has tried his best to keep from you —your God given blessing of success. Read, release, believe, and receive what Father God has for you.

SUCCESS

Success

"This book of the law shall not depart out of thy mouth; but thou shalt meditate therein day and night, that thou mayest observe to do according to all that is written therein: for then thou shalt make thy way prosperous, and then thou shalt have good success. Be strong and of good courage; be not afraid, neither be thou dismayed: for the Lord thy God is with thee whithersoever thou goest." Joshua 1:8-9

Poem

What does **Success** mean to me?

Success

Success Is climbing a MOUNTAIN ... reaching the TOP ... celebrating the MOMENT reaching back or down ... pulling others up ... and celebrating with them ... then MOVING to the NEXT LEVEL ... going HIGHER TOGETHER ... proceeding forward to HIGHER HEIGHTS ... leading the WAY ... as I follow the PATH.

Success is achieving something that I've set out to do and complete it. It is the completion of anything that I intended or planned to do.

Success is achieving my goals ... fulfilling my potential ... developing myself into a person who is valuable to others ... putting in 100% effort into what I'm doing so that it can come forth.

Success is consistently, steadily taking action and focusing my energy and efforts in the direction of what I'm aspiring to do or accomplish.

And finally, success breeds success. That means connecting with the right people at the right time, doing the right thing in the right place, and giving them full reign to take you where you want to go, with Christ (righteousness being the center) being our leader, and going THERE. WHERE? ... to SUCCESS.

JACQUELINE P. BROWN, Ph.D.

Chapter 1

---◆---

Life's Intruders

In July 2007, I encountered experiences in my life that were mind-boggling. There were manifestations of the hand of Satan revealed through many infallible proofs. After our 7th Holy Convocation, which was a great success, I received the shock of my real life. I say real because I had to be awakened to the real world of deceit, hypocrisy, and betrayal. I thought that love was with me and that it was great. You've not really loved until you love what doesn't love you. Deceit, hypocrisy, and betrayal. I was familiar with these words by reading the Holy Writ —The Bible.

I wasn't familiar with it through experiences, but I believe that God was saying you're now ready to know the TRUTH. You are at a place in ME that you will be able to STAND. "Wherefore take unto you the whole ARMOUR of GOD, that ye may be able to withstand in the evil day, and having done all, to stand. Stand therefore, having your loins girt about with TRUTH, and having on the BREASTPLATE of RIGHTEOUSNESS; And your feet shod with the preparation of the GOSPEL of PEACE; Above all, taking the SHIELD of FAITH, wherewith ye shall be able to quench all the fiery darts of the wicked.

And take the HELMET of SALVATION, and the SWORD of the SPIRIT, which is the WORD of GOD: PRAYING ALWAYS with all PRAYER and SUPPLICATION in the SPIRIT, and watching thereunto with all PERSEVERANCE and SUPPLICATION for all SAINTS" Ephesians 6:13-18.

God was ready for me to experience the TRUTH, which would propel me to higher heights and deeper depths in HIM, developing a greater Anointing in my life for the days ahead. God is always getting you ready for something greater. Wherever you are now, God is preparing you for something greater than where you are, so pay attention. Learn the lessons and record the events for future reference that will be occurring. There was a prophetic statement made prior to these experiences taking place in my life.

The prophetic word was, "There is going to be a turn of events in your life that will have a domino effect. They will be catastrophic." Have you ever had an inkling that something was brewing, but you just didn't know what it was or couldn't put your finger on it? Well, believe me, if you have then pay close attention to whatever your inkling is, look into it further because it just may not be an inkling. It just may be reality tapping at your door saying, "pay attention… pay attention… look… look… behold… behold."

Unaware of life's intruders comes confusion, trouble, chaos, and all other things that go along with that. When Satan enters or has an entrance, he brings other demonic spirits and forces with him.

In the Bible, you will find in the Book of Job, where Job was tested and tried. Job Chapter 1: verses 1-22 says, "There was a man in the land of Uz, whose name was Job; and that man was perfect and upright, and one that feared God, and eschewed evil. And there were born unto him seven sons and three daughters. His substance also was seven thousand sheep and three thousand camels, and five hundred yokes of oxen, and five hundred she asses, and a very great household; so that this man was the greatest of all the men of the east. And his sons went and feasted in their houses, and sent and called for their three sisters to eat and to drink with them.

And it was so, when the days of their feasting were gone about, that Job sent and sanctified them, and rose early in the morning, and offered burnt offerings according to the number of them all, for Job said, "It may be that my sons have sinned, and cursed God in their hearts." Thus, did Job continually.

Now there was a day when the sons of God came to present themselves before the Lord, and Satan came also among them. And the Lord said unto Satan, "Whence comest thou?" Then Satan answered the Lord and said, "From going to and fro in the earth and from walking up and down in it."

And the Lord said unto Satan, Hast thou considered my servant Job that there is none like him in the earth, a perfect and an upright man, one that feareth God, and escheweth evil?

Then Satan answered the Lord and said, "Doth Job fear God for nought? Hast not thou made an hedge about him, and about his house, and about all that he hath on every side? thou hast blessed the work of his hands, and his substance is increased in the land. But put forth thine hand now, and touch all that he hath, and he will curse thee to thy face." And the Lord said unto Satan, "Behold, all that he hath is in thy power; only upon himself put not forth thine hand."

So, Satan went forth from the presence of the Lord. And there was a day when his sons and daughters were eating and drinking wine in their eldest brother's house. And there came a messenger unto Job, and said, "The oxen were plowing, and the asses feeding beside them, and the Sabeans fell upon them and took them away; yea, they have slain the servants with the edge of the sword; and I only am escaped alone to tell thee. While he was yet speaking, there also came another, and said, "The fire of God is fallen from heaven, and hath burned up the sheep, and the servants, and consumed them, and I only am escaped alone to tell thee."

While he was yet speaking, there also came another, and said, The Chaldeans made out three bands, and fell upon the camels, and have carried them away, yea, and slain the servants with the edge of the sword; and I only am escaped alone to tell thee. While he was yet speaking, there also came another and said,

"Thy sons and thy daughters were eating and drinking wine in their eldest brother's house: And, behold, there came a great wind from the wilderness and smote the four corners of the house, and it fell upon the young men, and they are dead, and I only am escaped alone to tell thee.

Then Job arose, and rent his mantle, and shaved his head, and fell down upon the ground, and worshipped, and said, "Naked came I out of my mother's womb, and naked shall I return thither, the Lord gave, and the Lord hath taken away: blessed be the name of the Lord. In all this Job sinned not, nor charged God foolishly". Now just reading, looking, and hearing this story, we can see that this man named Job was perfect and an upright man. One that feared God and eschewed evil.

We also see, hear, and read that he had seven sons and three daughters. His substance was great. He had seven thousand sheep, three thousand camels, five hundred yokes of oxen, five hundred she asses, a great household, and was the greatest of all men of the east. This man is wealthy and rich, wanting nothing. Just because you think you have it all, you are not untouchable whether you are spiritually wealthy, materialistically wealthy, or financially wealthy. You are not untouchable. Life has a way of allowing things to happen in your life that brings reality into your present situation, and realness sets in.

If you want to be honest and above board, everyone is only seconds away from poverty. Job's sons and daughters were wealthy kids. Their father was wealthy, and therefore they could eat, drink, and be merry anytime they wanted to, for some children they would think this is the Life.

However, this is a facade. This appears to be life. This appears to be living, but this is not life, and this is not living. **Life is in Christ**. Job sons went and feasted in their houses, everyone his day and sent and called for their three sisters to eat and drink with them. You can imagine what eating and drinking men and women will do, and these were sisters and brothers with each other and possibly a whole lot of sexual perversion taking place unknowingly. When their days of feasting were finished, Job sent for them and sanctified them, and got up early in the morning and offered burnt offerings according to the number of them all for fear that the sons had sinned and cursed God in their hearts. Not outwardly but inwardly.

Job seemingly had to be a man of God who really had a heart for God. And all he wanted for his family was to have respect and a love for God. But as usual, you hear the saying," children will be children." Yes, they will, but children that are taught morally and children who are taught the ways of the Lord stand a better chance of making better moral and right decisions.

To drink is not a good decision, for it interferes with your capacity to think logically and ultimately destroys your health. For brothers to invite their sisters while eating and drinking after a few days is not logically correct because anything could take place that you regret later. Incest. But who cares? Let's eat, drink, and be merry. You ask, who cares? The father cared. The one who was perfect and upright, the one who feared God and eschewed evil. Job cared for himself and for his children. Job has the awesome responsibility of standing in the gap for his children. You say he doesn't have to do that. As long as the children are home or around or near the home, and you know of their actions, you as a parent of that child or children are still responsible for teaching that child or children correctly and standing in the gap.

However, we know that children at the age of 12 or 13 become responsible for their own actions, whether good or bad. Children are a blessing and therefore are to be treated as such. So Job does what he can do. He gives good parental guidance.

Now everybody thinks everything is okay but not so. When you think that everything is okay, and you have it going on, watch out and look carefully because Satan is waiting for an entrance. Life's intruders are lurking to dismantle your hookey doorey day.

Now there was a day when the sons of God came to present themselves before the Lord, and Satan also came among them. You might ask why was Satan there? He was not invited. But Satan presents himself as an angel of light continuously II Corinthians11:14.

How many times do you invite the good and the evil shows up? It's life's intruders. Something or someone who has come to rob you of your life. ***Jesus said, "I am come that they might have life, and that they might have it more abundantly"*** St. John 10:10b It is your choice. Deuteronomy 30:19-20 says, "I call heaven and earth to record this day against you, that I have set before you *life* and death, *blessing* and cursing: therefore *choose life, that both thou and thy seed may live:* That thou mayest love the Lord thy God, and that thou mayest obey HIS voice, and that thou mayest cleave unto HIM: for **HE is thy LIFE** and *the length of thy days*: that thou mayest dwell in the land which the Lord swore unto thy fathers, to Abraham, to Isaac, and to Jacob, to give them" ***It is your choice.***

Yet the thief comes to steal, kill, and destroy. St. John 10:10a says, "The thief cometh not, but for to steal and to kill, and to destroy" Notice the progression of the thief. First, the thief steals, then the thief kills, and ultimately the thief destroys. But ***Jesus gives life first and abundance next.*** So, there is no question of who is at work.

When you see these things happening in your life, you know who is in operation. Therefore, you know how to react to the prevalent situation. When you see these things happening in your life, you know who is present. If you then know who is present, you know what to do, and you will still continue to have life even in the midst of the entry of these life intruders.

The Lord said unto Satan, Whence comest thou? Then Satan answered the Lord, and said, From going to and fro in the earth, and from walking up and down in it. Now the Lord did not have to ask Satan anything but He did. For the Lord knew what Satan was doing and what he was all about.

Yet the Lord asked him the question, and Satan answered and gave a general evasive answer. Right there, we see deceit. And the Lord said unto Satan, Hast thou considered my servant Job, that there is none like him in the earth, a perfect and an upright man, one that feareth God and escheweth evil.

God is always looking for someone to put on display for Kingdom purposes, just as Satan is always looking for someone to disgrace. God is always ready to promote someone so that the Kingdom of God can move forward in the earth realm, just as Satan is looking for someone he can dethrone and takedown. God is looking for someone HE can bless more abundantly, just as Satan is looking for someone he can curse.

God already knows your character and is constantly developing more Christ-like character in you and will let everyone know HE knows your character, yet Satan knows your past, and Satan tries to get you to go back to your past but God knows your present and future and has thrown your past into the sea of forgetfulness and remembers it no more and Satan seemingly thinks that he can get you to go back to your past.

However, if you are with God, your past is passed. The question is, can God brag on you to Satan? Then Satan answered the Lord and said, "Doth Job fear God for nought?" In other words, Job is only serving you because of what YOU gave to him or what he possesses. Job does not fear YOU for nothing. It is because of what YOU have released to him and what YOU have loaned to him while here upon earth. He serves you for the fish and five loaves of bread.

Job is blessed. YOU blessed him, and he serves YOU because of the blessing. Hast not thou made a hedge about him, and about his house, and about all that he hath on every side? Thou hast blessed the work of his hands, and his substance is increased in the land.

Look at this picture. Satan literally tells what he is going to attack. Satan sees the blessings of God on and in Job's life, and therefore knows that if these things and blessings are removed from Job's life, he can have access to Job's life and begin his evil work on and in Job's life.

Divine Protection, material Possessions, and occupation. Life's intruders are brought by Satan to afflict all that God has blessed you with. He literally tells what he sees God has blessed Job with and this is what he wants to remove from Job's life so that he can prove to God that Job serves God because of the blessings of God in and on Job's life.

Satan is also ready to prove to God that if the blessings are removed from your life, he would be able to turn you away from the" KING of kings" and the" LORD of lords." The question is, can Satan do that to you?

Now Satan challenges God and says, "But put forth thine hand now, and touch all that he hath, and he will curse thee to thy face. Man, this guy is something. This force of evil is challenging the one who controls POWER. And the Lord said unto Satan, Behold, all that he hath is in thy power; only upon himself put not forth thine hand. So, Satan went forth from the presence of the Lord because he now has been given access. He's been given the assignment to try and test Job.

Satan can't do anything to you unless he gets permission from God. If God is placing you on display for Kingdom purposes, God will take care of you. God challenged Satan, and then Satan challenged God using Job as their person of the challenge. Are you being tested today? Are you going through some trying times? Is your back against the wall? You then are on display. You've been challenged.

Chapter 2

The Challenges of Life/Job

Now the Lord has given Satan permission to attack Job. And, of course, Satan is happy because now he gets the chance he's been waiting for to make Job turn on God. But he doesn't understand God would have never given Satan permission if He knew Job wasn't going to stand up to the challenge and challenges of life.

Challenges are not easy, but if you're really with Christ, He will fortify you for the fight. Job was ready to "Fight the good fight of FAITH, lay hold on eternal life, whereunto thou art also called, and hast professed a good profession before many witnesses" James chapter 6 verse 12 Are you getting this?

Job did this. Job's life did this. You did this. Your life did this. You proclaimed Jesus Christ before a great cloud of witnesses now. Satan wants and is trying to get you to denounce Christ before these same clouds of witnesses and more. The devil is a lie and a liar. God's been so good to you and to me that we must stand the challenges of life, and this challenge must not go unnoticed.

It came, but it came to pass. It has come our way, and we must face it. We must confront it. We must not run. We all face challenges in our lives, knowing that God can perfect something in our lives even more for HIS GLORY and for HIS HONOR, in Jesus Name. In fact, God has already fortified you for the fight ahead through something you have already been doing. You were just not aware of what was happening in your spiritual walk with Christ. You are already ready for the fight. You just don't know it, but God does. That's why it has come. "Count it all joy when ye fall into diverse temptations; knowing this, that the trying of your FAITH worketh patience. But let patience have her perfect work, that ye may be perfect and entire, wanting nothing" James chapter 1 verses 2-4.

And now that Satan has been given permission, he does not miss a beat. He begins his attacks. Yes, I said attacks because he comes with more than one. Job now has to embrace the fight ahead, not knowing the conversation God and Satan had concerning his life. So here goes the fight. And there was a day when his sons and daughters were eating and drinking wine in their eldest brother's house:

And there came a messenger unto Job, and said, "The oxen were plowing, and the asses feeding beside them: And the Sabeans fell upon them, and took them away; yea, they have slain the servants with the edge of the sword; and I only am escaped alone to tell thee." Oh, my God, this must have been devastating. Five hundred oxen and five hundred asses. That's a lot of wealth. That's a loss of wealth. That's a **loss of income**.

Oh well, let me get over that at least the camels and sheep and all other things are in tack. Thank you so much for coming to tell me. While he was yet speaking, there also came another, and said, "The fire of God is fallen from heaven, and hath burned up the sheep, and the servants, and consumed them; and I only am escaped alone to tell thee." Oh, my Lord, seven thousand sheep what am I going to do?

That's **more wealth**. That's more livestock. Well, I still have the camels. I'll make it. It will be alright. Thank you so much for coming to tell me. While he was yet speaking, there also came another, and said, "The Chaldeans made out three bands, and fell upon the camels, and have carried them away, yea, and slain the servants with the edge of the sword; and I only am escaped alone to tell thee." Oh, Jesus, what am I going to do?

All income is gone now. All wealth is depleted. Jesus, Jesus, Jesus, help me three thousand camels, please help me, please help me. Okay, okay, I still have ***family,*** and we can work together and achieve again. It may take a little while, but we can accomplish it. We can accomplish it once we can do it again. Okay, okay, okay, thank you so much for coming and telling me what happened. While he was yet speaking, there also came another, and said, "Thy sons and thy daughters were eating and drinking wine in their eldest brother's house; And, behold, there came a great wind from the wilderness, and smote the four corners of the house, and it fell upon the young men, and they are dead, and I only am escaped alone to tell thee." This is it. Oh, my Lord, where are You, Lord? Where are You? Help me, help me, Oh Jesus!

Four attacks Satan launched. Four messengers left to tell the story. God is going to always have someone to tell the story. God is always going to protect someone so that they will be able to tell the story. No matter what Satan is doing, there is **DIVINE PROTECTION** for those who will tell the story. God is going to protect Job, and God is going to protect the messengers. The messengers are the witnesses to tell the story. Satan attacked four places, **Wealth, Income, Material Possessions, and Family.**

This is what he does because he believes this is what you live for. He believes that this is what's close to you. He thinks this is what makes you tick.

Now at one point in your life, these things were probably true, and Satan thought that this was still true. However, Satan deals with your past. God deals with your present and your future. Are you getting this? When Job heard all these sayings, then Job arose, and rent his mantle, shaved his head, and fell upon the ground, ***and worshipped***. It is evident that Job was in a sitting position when all these previous occurrences took place, and none of those things really moved him, but when it hit family, it hit home.

This moved him to another posture. Family moved him. It hit inside the camp. Inside the door. It hit his heart (*Z*). So, what do you do when it hits home? When it hits family? ***The 1st posture was he arose***. Got to get up now, and he got up.

This is a bit much. I *must prepare for* a *battle*. He rent his mantle (his robe). This is *the 2nd posture;* this is an all-out battle. He shaved his head. This is *the 3rd posture*. Get rid of everything. He fell down. This is *the 4th posture.* Humility. Come on, Jesus. I need You. I need Your help. I went as far as I could go with the anointing that was given. Now, I need more. More for this journey ahead. Please anoint me even more. Come on, Jesus. He fell down upon the ground, and the *5th posture HE WORSHIPPED. Worshipped*?

Yes **WORSHIPPED.** That's what you do when the attacks of Satan come to you one right after another. You worship God even the More. **WORSHIP, PRAY, and PRAISE.** Praise God!!! God, I *worship* You in spite of. You see, Satan is after your *worship* of God. Remember Satan said he would make Job curse God to HIS face. And that's what Satan is trying to do with you and me. But Satan is a liar. Greater is HE that is in me, and you than he that is in the world. **PRAYER** changes things. **Humility** brings salvation and more things. And **WORSHIP** is the place where HE (God) wants me and you to be and to go. So, despite of what it looks like and of what it seems, it is where GOD wants you and me in **WORSHIP with HIM.** He wants our undistracted and undivided attention.

Okay, God, I get the picture. You are up to something. I am being set up for a push up in more ways than one. It's elevation time. It's promotion time. It's a blessing time. When the enemy attacked in July 2007 in my life, at a point, I thought I had defeated the enemy by canceling his assignment when he tried to hurt the vision God had given regarding the people of God for that season. And I was determined that God's Program would continue in the Light of Jesus Christ and not satanic atmospheres. "For the weapons of our warfare are not carnal, but mighty through God to the pulling down of strongholds; Casting down imaginations, and every high thing that exalteth itself against the knowledge of God, and bringing into captivity every thought to the obedience of Christ; And having in a readiness to revenge all disobedience, when your obedience is fulfilled." II Corinthians 10th chapter verses 4-6.

But the enemy is not going down without a fight. He is going to fight, and you must fight back. The way he fights is different from the way we fight. The enemy fights with lies. You then must fight with truth. The enemy fights with stealing, and you then must fight with giving no matter how small. Just keep giving of yourself and of your substance.

You must remember that Satan is under your feet. You are still in charge. You just have to make sure that you follow righteousness no matter what comes. As a Pastor, you are to lead the parishioners in the ways of Christ. You can't make them, but you lead them. If they do not follow, that is their decision. You just make sure you lead them in the ways of the Lord through HIS HOLY WRIT and, as best as possible, give them an example life of Christ. You are not God, but God is in you, and you are to exemplify as much as possible to where your life is in Christ, **the Life of Christ**.

He has no hands or feet but ours. We are HIS ambassadors in the earth realm. "Therefore, if any man be in Christ, he is a new creature: old things are passed away; behold, all things are become new. And all things are of God, who hath reconciled us to HIMSELF by Jesus Christ, and hath given to us the ***ministry of reconciliation***; To wit, that God was in Christ, reconciling the world unto HIMSELF, not imputing their trespasses unto them; and hath committed unto us ***the word of reconciliation***. Now then we are Ambassadors for Christ, as though God did beseech you by us: we pray you in Christ's stead, be ye reconciled to God. For HE hath made HIM to be sin for us, who knew no sin; that we might be made the righteousness of God in HIM". II Corinthians, 6th chapter verses 17-21.

July 2007 was most devastating in my life because it did start the attacks of the enemy in my life to try to make me give up, to throw in the towel, and to leave the ministry.

However, I kept hearing a still small voice telling me it's going to be alright. "You can make it, keep going for I am with you." I kept hearing positive words of encouragement, and having a ministry. A Church that was once thriving and moving with the ways of the Lord. All of a sudden manifest the story in Bible that says, "Another parable he put forth unto them, saying, "The kingdom of heaven is likened unto a man which sowed good seed in his field:

But while men slept, his enemy came and sowed tares among the wheat and went his way. But when the blade was sprung up and brought forth fruit, then appeared the tares also. So, the servants of the householder came and said unto him, "Sir, didst not thou sow good seed in thy field? From whence then hath it tares?" He said unto them, "An enemy hath done this. The servants said unto him, wilt thou then that we go and gather them up?" But he said, "Nay; lest while ye gather up the tares ye root up also the wheat with them. Let both grow together until the harvest: and in the time of harvest I will say to the reapers, "Gather ye together first the tares, and bind them in bundles to burn them: but gather the wheat into my barn" St. Matthew, 13th chapter verses 24-30.

You see, when you have sown **the WORD of GOD,** then you let God handle everything, for if God's Word can't do it in a person's life, then nothing else can. God's Word is powerful. "For the Word of God is quick, and powerful, and sharper than any two-edged sword, piercing even to the dividing asunder of soul and spirit, and of the joints and marrow, and is a discerner of the thoughts and intents of the heart." Hebrews 4th chapter verse 12.

God will do it. Let God handle it. It will be alright. You just keep going forward, not looking back. "No man, having put his hand to the plough, and looking back, is fit for the Kingdom of God." St. Luke, chapter 9 verse 62.

Letting go of everything and anything that does not want to continue the walk of Christ with you. Keep going forward and watch the move of God. "But as it is written, Eye hath not seen, nor ear heard neither have entered into the heart of man, the things which God hath prepared for them that love HIM." I Corinthians, Chapter 2 verse 9.

Now let's continue our story. Job **Worshiped,** and that's what it takes. **Worship!!!** Notice Job's Worship to God. He said, Naked came I out of my mother's womb, and naked shall I return thither: The Lord gave, and the Lord hath taken away; blessed be the name of the Lord. Job recognizes that he came here with nothing and he shall leave, taking nothing with him and acknowledges that everything he had God gave it to him, and since God gave it to him, God has the right to do with what HE gave to him whatever HE wants to do. God gave God can take away.

Nevertheless, blessed be the name of the Lord. Now can you do this? Can you let go no matter what, knowing that whatever God has given, HE has the right to take away and then bless HIS HOLY NAME? Because this is the way out of your dilemma. This is the way toward *your next miracle*. This is the way to *the next dimension*. This is the way to *a greater anointing*. This is the way. **Worship!!!** This is the path. **Worship!!!** Walk therein. **Worship!!!** In all this, Job sinned not, nor charged God foolishly.

So, what the devil meant for evil, God turns it to be good. *Job passed the test of wealth, material possessions, income, family,* and everything that goes along with those things. But God knew that Job would **Worship HIM** despite of and **bless HIS HOLY NAME.** God knew, and Satan didn't know. Did you get that? And you are being challenged today. Right now, God knows what you will do and how you will respond, while Satan does not know.

When these attacks of Satan hit in my life, I continued to seek the Word of God for *refuge and guidance*. In the scripture, it speaks of a parable that was significant. "Behold, a sower went forth to sow; and when he sowed, some seeds fell by the wayside, and the fowls came and devoured them up:

Some fell upon stony places, where they had not much earth: and forthwith they sprung up because they had no deepness of earth: And when the sun was up, they were scorched; and because they had no root they withered away. And some fell among thorns, and the thorns sprung up, and choked them: But other fell into **good ground**, and **brought forth fruit**, some a **hundredfold**, some *sixtyfold*, some *thirtyfold.* Who hath ears to hear, let him hear." St. Matthew, 13 Chapter verses 19-23.

To explain it better, "Hear ye, therefore, the parable of the sower. When anyone heareth the **WORD of the KINGDOM**, and understandeth it not, then cometh the wicked one, and catcheth away that which was sown in his heart. This is he, who received seed by the wayside. But he that received the seed into stony places, the same is he that heareth the WORD, and anon with joy receiveth it; Yet hath he not roots in himself but dureth for a while: for when tribulation or persecution ariseth because of the WORD, by and by he is offended. He also that received seed among the thorns is he that heareth the WORD; and the care of this world, and the deceitfulness of riches, choke the WORD and he becometh unfruitful. But he that received seed into the good ground is he that heareth the WORD, and understandeth it; which also beareth fruit, and bringeth forth, some a hundredfold, some sixty, some thirty. So, for those that were good ground, fruit will come up thirty, sixty, and a hundredfold no matter where they are and ***to God be all the GLORY.***

Chapter 3

The Attacks of the Enemy

The attacks of Satan were very strong after I canceled the assignment of the enemy. He then began to move about with first one thing and then another. It began with an attack, after attack, after attack. Starting with a wrong word spoken in secret, a wrong action triggered openly, and the blind now leading the blind. What a catastrophe. What a hurt for some 20 years invested, looking as though it has gone down the drain.

However, I kept my focus on God and my trust in God's ability to move on our behalf. I began to ask what is God trying to prove to me and to others? Negative words coming out of the mouths that at one time was under my tutelage. Shunned by persons I thought were my friends. Laugh at and abandoned by those who were once I thought with us. People you confided in. I am then reminded of the disciples of Christ. How Jesus taught, led, loved, and cared for the disciples and then one betrayed, another denied, and others ran.

People that I thought I could trust and move God's ministry forward no longer present, and I was left with a challenge of the vision coming forth with a remnant of persons. A congregational split. How often do we feel we are leading persons correctly through the Word of God and anticipating great things for them in the Kingdom to find out you were just training them for someone else? But Jesus said, I will never leave you, I will never forsake you. Hebrews 13: 5.

Looking at the story of Gideon, Judges chapter 6-chapter 8. "And the children of Israel did evil in the sight of the Lord: and the Lord delivered them into the hand of Midian seven years. And the hand of the Midian prevailed against Israel: and because of the Midianites the children of Israel made them the dens which are in the mountains, and caves, and strongholds. And so it was, when Israel had sown, that the Midianites came up, and the Amalekites, and the children of the east, even they came up against them; And they encamped against them, and destroyed the increase of the earth, till thou come unto Gaza, and left no sustenance for Israel, neither sheep, nor ox, nor ass. For they came up with their cattle and their tents, and they came as grasshoppers for multitude; for both they and their camels were without number: and they entered into the land to destroy it. And Israel was greatly impoverished because of the Midianites, **and the children of Israel cried unto the Lord.** And it came to pass when the children of Israel cried unto the Lord because of the Midianites, That ***the Lord sent a prophet*** unto the children of Israel, ***which said unto them, "Thus saith the Lord God of Israel, I brought you up from Egypt, and brought you forth out of the house of bondage; And I delivered you out of the hand of the Egyptians, and out of the hand of all that oppressed you, and drave them out from before you, and gave you their land;" And I said unto you, I am the Lord your God; fear not the gods of the Amorites, in whose land ye dwell: but ye have not obeyed my voice. And there came an angel of the Lord, and sat under an oak which was in Ophrah,*** that pertained unto Joash the Abiezrite: and his son Gideon threshed wheat by the winepress, to hide it from the Midianites. ***And the angel of the Lord appeared unto him, and said unto him, The Lord is with thee, thou mighty man of valour.***

And Gideon said unto him, Oh, my Lord, if the Lord be with us, why then is all this befallen us? And where be all his miracles which our fathers told us of saying, "Did not the Lord bring us up from Egypt? But now the Lord hath forsaken us, and delivered us into the hands of the Midianites. *And the Lord looked upon him and said, Go, in this thy might, and thou shall save Israel from the hand of the Midianites: have not I sent thee?"* And he said unto him, "Oh my lord, wherewith shall I save Israel? Behold, my family is poor in Manasseh, and I am the least in my father's house." *And the Lord said unto him, "Surely I will be with thee, and thou shalt smite the Midianites as one man."* And he said unto him, "*If now I have found grace* in thy sight, then shew me a sign that thou talkest with me. Depart not thence, I pray thee, until I come unto thee, and bring forth my present, and set it before thee. *And he said, I will tarry until thou come again."*

And Gideon went in, and made ready a kid and unleavened cakes of an ephah of flour: the flesh he put in a basket, and put the broth in a pot, and brought it out unto him under the oak, and presented it. *And the angel of God said unto him, Take the flesh and the unleavened cakes, and lay them upon this rock, and pour out the broth.* And he did so. *Then the angel of the Lord put forth the end of the staff that was in his hand, and touched the flesh and the unleavened cakes, and there rose up fire out of the rock and consumed the flesh and the unleavened cakes. Then the angel of the Lord departed out of his sight.* And when Gideon perceived that he was an angel of the Lord, Gideon said, Alas, O Lord God! for because I have seen an angel of the Lord face to face. *And the Lord said unto him, "Peace be unto thee; fear not: thou shalt not die."* Then Gideon built an altar there unto the Lord and **called it Jehovah-Shalom: which means, The Lord our Peace** unto this day it is yet in Ophrah of the Abiezrites. *And it came to pass the same night, that the Lord said unto him, Take thy father's young bullock, even the second bullock of seven years old, and throw down the altar of Baal that thy father hath, and cut down the grove that is by it: And build an altar unto the Lord thy God upon the top of this rock, in the ordered place, and take the second bullock, and offer a burnt sacrifice with the wood of the grove which thou shalt cut down.*

Then Gideon took ten men of his servants and did as the Lord had said unto him: and so, it was, because he feared his father's household, and the men of the city, that he could not do it by day, that he did it by night. And when the men of the city arose early in the morning, behold, the altar of Baal was cast down, and the grove was cut down that was by it, and the second bullock was offered upon the altar that was built. And they said one to another, who hath done this thing? And when they inquired and asked, they said, Gideon the son of Joash hath done this thing. Then the men of the city said unto Joash, bring out thy son that he may die: because he hath cast down the altar of Baal and because he hath cut down the grove that was by it.

And Joash said unto all that stood against him, Will ye plead for Baal? Will ye save him? he that will plead for him, let him be put to death whilst it is yet morning: if he be a god, let him plead for himself, because one hath cast down his altar. Therefore, on that day he called him Jerubbaal, saying, "Let Baal pleads against him, because he hath thrown down his altar."

Then all the Midianites and the Amalekites and the children of the east were gathered together, and went over, and pitched in the valley of Jezreel. **But the Spirit of the Lord came upon Gideon, and he blew a trumpet,** and Abiezer was gathered after him. And he sent messengers throughout all Manassah; who also was gathered after him: and he sent messengers unto Asher, and unto Zebulun, and unto Naphtali, and they came up to meet them.

And Gideon said unto God, If thou wilt save Israel by mine hand, as thou hast said, Behold, I will put a fleece of wool in the floor; and if the dew be on the fleece only, and it be dry upon all the earth beside, then shall I know that thou wilt save Israel by mine hand, as thou hast said. And it was so: for he rose up early on the morrow, and thrust the fleece together, and wringed the dew out of the fleece, a bowl full of water.

And Gideon said unto God, "Let not thine anger be hot against me, and I will speak but this once: let me prove, I pray thee, but this once with the fleece; let it now be dry only upon the fleece, and upon all the ground let there be dew." And God did so that night, for it was dry upon the fleece only, and there was dew on all the ground. As we look at this, we see a pattern.

the children of Israel cried unto the Lord . . . verse 6
the Lord sent a Prophet . . . verses 8-10
then an Angel of the Lord appeared . . . verses 11-16
A request of a sign . . . verse 17
Gideon gives a present/an offering . . . verses 18-19
A sign given . . . verses 20-22
Gideon acknowledges the Angel . . . verse 22
A blessing is given . . . verse 23
Prayer and Praise rendered . . . verse 24
Instructions given . . . verses 25-26
Obedience to the instructions . . . verse 27
Destruction of idol god
Evidence of idol god destroyed . . . verse 28
Confrontation . . . verses 29-31
The Challenge . . . verses 31-33
The Presence/The Spirit of the Lord/The Anointing . . . verse 34
A sign requested . . . verse 36
A sign given . . . verse 38
Another sign requested . . . verse 39
Another sign given . . . verse 40

When you cry out unto the Lord, He will answer. But your cry must be a fervent cry. An I need You Lord.
Please come see about me. And the Lord will send you a prophetic word . . . the presence of an angelic being such as the illumination of light may present itself and the Spirit of the Lord will speak to your spirit and give Divine Instructions. At this point your faith must kick in. Whomever brought or gave the Prophetic Word, you are to give an offering or do something special for them and a blessing will be placed upon you. You then render Prayer and Praise to God and instructions will be given. Obey the instructions. Destroy the idol. Cast down every evil imagination that will set itself up above

the will of God. Destroy the devil in your life. Bring him/ bring it down. Now when you do this there will be confrontation. The challenge . . . but the Presence of the Lord/The Spirit of the Most High/ The Anointing will rest upon you and overshadow you and nothing shall by any means hurt or harm you. You're then in Victory mode . . . Stay focused!!! Let your faith kick in!!!

Looking at Chapter Seven of Judges we can see the work of the Lord even clearer.

Then Jerubbaal, who is Gideon, and all the people that were with him, rose early, and pitched beside the well of Harod: so that the host of the Midianites were on the north side of them, by the hill of Moreh, in the valley. *And the Lord said unto Gideon, the people that are with thee are too many for me to give the Midianites into their hands, lest Israel vaunt themselves against Me, saying, mine own hand hath saved me. Now, therefore, go to, proclaim in the ears of the people, saying, whoever is fearful and afraid, let him return and depart early from mount Gilead, And there returned of the people twenty and two thousand; and there remained ten thousand.*

And the Lord said unto Gideon, "The people are yet too many, bring them down unto the water, and I will try them for thee there: and it shall be, that of whom I say unto thee, This shall go with thee, the same shall go with thee; and of whomsoever I say unto thee, This shall not go with thee, the same shall not go.

And the Lord said unto Gideon, "Everyone that lappeth of the water with his tongue, as a dog lappeth, him shalt thou set by himself; likewise, everyone that boweth down upon his knees to drink."

And the number of them that lapped, putting their hand to their mouth, were three hundred men: but all the rest of the people bowed down upon their knees to drink water. *And the LORD said unto Gideon, By the three hundred men that lapped will I save you, and deliver the Midianites into thine hand: and let all the other people go every man unto his place.*

So, the people took victuals in their hand, and their trumpets: and he sent all the rest of Israel every man unto his tent, and retained those three hundred men: and the host of Midian was beneath him in the valley. And it came to pass the same night, that ***the Lord said unto him, Arise, get thee down unto the host; for I have delivered it into thine hand. But if thou fear to go down, go thou with Phurah thy servant down to the host: And thou shalt hear what they say; and afterward shall thine hands be strengthened to go down unto the host.***

Then went he down with Phurah, his servant unto the outside of the armed men that were in the host. And the Midianites and the Amalekites and all the children of the east lay along in the valley like grasshoppers for multitude; and their camels were without number, as the sand by the seaside for multitude. And when Gideon was come, behold, there was a man that told a dream unto his fellow, and said, Behold, I dreamed a dream, and, lo, a cake of barley bread tumbled into the host of Midian, and came unto a tent, and smote it that it fell, and overturned it, that the tent lay along. And his fellow answered and said, *"This is nothing else save the **sword of Gideon** the son of Joash, a man of Israel: for **into his hand hath God delivered Midian, and all the host.***

And *it was so*, when Gideon heard the telling of the dream, and the interpretation thereof, that ***he worshipped,*** and returned into the host of Israel, and said, *"**Arise for the Lord hath delivered into your hand the host of Midian." And he divided the three hundred men into three companies, and he put a trumpet in every man's hand, with empty pitchers, and lamps within the pitchers. And he said unto them, "look on me, and do likewise: and behold, when I come to the outside of the camp, it shall be that, as I do, so shall ye do. When I blow with a trumpet, I and all that are with me, then blow ye the trumpets also on every side of all the camp and say, "The sword of the Lord and of Gideon."*

So, Gideon, and the hundred men that were with him, came unto the outside of the camp at the beginning of the middle watch (midnight); and they had but newly set the watch: and they blew the trumpets, and brake the pitchers that were in their hands. And the three companies **blew the trumpets**, and **brake the pitchers**, and held the lamps in their left hands, and the trumpets in their right hands to blow withal: and **they cried, The sword of the Lord, and of Gideon.**

And they stood every man in his place round about the camp: and all the host ran, and cried, and fled. And the three hundred blew the trumpets, and the Lord set every man's sword against his fellow, even throughout all the host: and the host fled to Bethshittah in Zererath, and to the border of Abelmeholah, unto Tabbath.

God will handle your enemies; you don't ever have to fight. The battle is not yours. It's the Lord's. And He will accomplish that He set out to do. He just uses you to carry out HIS program. Count it a privilege to be used for the Kingdom of God. Remember: "All things come of THEE Oh LORD and of THINE OWN have we given THEE."

God wants the credit!
Go wants to get the credit and HE is going to get it!
God wants to bless you!
God wants to get the GLORY!
God wants to get the HONOR!
God wants you to testify about HIM!
God wants you to testify about HIS WONDROUS WORKS!
Notice the pattern!
You must first rid yourself of those who are fearful!
You must rid yourself of those who are afraid!

This is a separation, a division. Let them go back home, for the Scripture has said, he who putteth his hand to the plow looking back is not fit for the Kingdom. Now Gideon is left with ten thousand out of thirty-two thousand. This is separation, and division is for the blessing to come forth. Because faith and fear don't go together, they don't mix. It takes faith with faith and fear with fear, and each will accomplish what they set out to do to either go forward or to go back. Either to accomplish or to fail believers with believers and unbelievers with unbelievers, and I am sure you are getting the picture. A leader must have followers even if the followers don't understand the entire picture. They must be able to receive instructions and move with their leader.

Sometimes you think you need an army, but with God, you just need what God says. God is downsizing for the VICTORY.

Look at this again. First, it was the spoken word. Secondly, the test, the trial by God in order to observe, in order for Gideon to know beyond a shadow of a doubt who God wanted to use for the VICTORY because God already knew HE's GOD, ALL KNOWING, OMNISCIENT. And thirdly the right number, the number that will obey the instructions of God through the leader without question, the number that will trust God and believe that the VICTORY is at hand. And lastly, look at this next thing they are given provisions and an instrument. Oh, the heat is on now. It's on now. God has the number of people HE is going to use now. God must fortify the leader more for the FIGHT of FAITH.

You see, it is a FAITH FIGHT. So, God fortifies the leader and instructs him that if he needs help to go the distance get someone he can trust, saying if you fear, go with someone you can trust, and Gideon takes his servant. As he goes down into the enemy's camp, Gideon hears a dream and the interpretation of it, and Gideon worshipped.

You say WORSHIP. YES, WORSHIP. You must WORSHIP. This is the key to your VICTORY. RESPECT GOD. REVERENCE GOD. God is the one through whom this VICTORY is going to come forth. Now Gideon was the leader, and once he received a word from God of VICTORY, he gave instructions to the three hundred of VICTORY.

Obedience is another key to your VICTORY. Obedience to GOD, and to those who have rule over you. You must declare war and go with GOD. IT's a Fight. It's the battle of Faith in GOD. the leader is ready, and the followers are ready. The FIGHT is ON. They now blow the trumpets and break the pitchers and cried, "The sword of the Lord and of Gideon." Yes, that's what they did. They did what they were instructed to do by their leader as God being the CHIEF LEADER.

You see, the enemy makes you afraid and fearful and presents you with the impossible, and yes, with you, it is impossible, but with God, all things are possible. WITH GOD, ALL THINGS ARE POSSIBLE. As Gideon and the three hundred blew the trumpets and broke the pitchers and said the sword of the Lord and of Gideon, the enemy runs, cries, and flees. PRAISE THE LORD. THE BATTLE IS WON. THE VICTORY IS ACCOMPLISHED. GOD DID IT! The Lord Manifest the Victory and to HIM be all GLORY AND HONOR, AMEN!!

Chapter 4

Motives Defined

How often do we feel or think we're leading someone correctly and anticipating great things for them in the Kingdom to find out that wasn't it after all? That their motives were much different than yours. You remember the Tower of Babel. The tower of Babel was a place where God confounded the language. For at one time, the earth was of one language, which denoted great unity.

However, they decided they would build a city and a tower that would lead from earth to heaven, and God decided to confuse the language because He said if He didn't, they would accomplish what they set out to do, but that wasn't what God had for them. Their motives were much different from God's motive. God knows the value of UNITY. In Genesis 11th chapter verses 1-9.

And the whole earth was of **one language,** and **one speech.** And it came to pass, as they journeyed from the east, that they found a plain in the land of Shinar; and they dwelt there. And they said one to another, "Go to, let us make brick, and burn them thoroughly." And they had brick for stone, and slime had them for mortar. And *they said, "Go to, let us build us a city and a tower, whose top may reach unto heaven; and let* *us make us a name, lest we be scattered abroad upon the face of the whole earth."* And the Lord came down to see the city and the tower, which the children of men build. And **the Lord said, *"Behold, the people is one, and they have all one language; and this they begin to do: and now nothing will be restrained from them, which they have imagined to do. Go to, let us go down, and there confound their language, that they may not understand one another's speech."***

So, the Lord scattered them abroad from thence upon the face of all the earth: and they left off to build the city. Therefore, is the name of it called Babel; because the Lord did there confound the language of all the earth: and from thence did the Lord scatter them abroad upon the face of all the earth. Because their motives were not right. God never intended for them to build a city and a tower whose top would reach heaven. God never intended for them to make a name for themselves. God never intended for them to be unified in wrong motives.

Your motives must be right. Your motives must be Godly. Your motives must be in the Divine Will of God. Now the devil knows the results of division and disunity from the will of God. ***Unsuccessful! This is confusion, chaos, separation, and division from God.***

Also, how many times have you confided in a person because of the Word of God saying, "Confess your faults one to another, and pray one for another, that ye may be healed. The effectual fervent prayer of a righteous man availeth much" James 5:16 and yet they turned and deceived you? Wow, that's a kick. What a catastrophe! Being opened, honest, and transparent and they turned and deceived you. You see this is crazy because this is not the way of persons who have integrity. You know to talk to God but what earthly person can you talk to and be healed?

A righteous person, not a self-righteous person. God will, through the Power of the Holy Spirit, put or place someone in your life that you can confide in and be opened and honest with so that you may be healed. Healing is the children's bread. Healing is coming to your house now. Healing is coming to you in the name of Jesus. Are you anticipating and expecting great things, and all of a sudden, you're introduced to the real world?

Dreams shattered, confronting challenges you did not anticipate and seemingly unprepared for. Daggers being plunged, wounds being opened and hurt inevitably.

Steady your course. God is with you. He said, "He will never leave you," He will never forsake you. Blessings are on the way. You may not see them now because of your present seemingly rough situation but stay focused because you're being channel for greatness.

Let me tell you of an experience I once had. I received one day after a great service a letter from one of the parishioners of the church expressing their desire to leave the ministry to further advance in the Kingdom. At this point, I am a little baffled because I believe that this individual would be mightily used in the present local assembly and then mightier abroad.

I respond to the contents of the letter by questioning them and then give insight to them to the will of God as discerned by me. But to no avail. Seeing the determination of their decision to leave, I then ask who is going with you? How many are you taking? I've always noticed that for some apparent reason, those who leave never leave alone. They always take someone with them. Now, this may not have been the intention, but it was the response that was received. Remember Abram? Genesis 12th chapter verses 1-4a.

Now the Lord had said unto Abram, Get thee out of thy country, and from thy kindred and from thy father's house, unto a land that I will shew thee: And I will make of thee a great nation, and I will bless thee, and make thy name great; and thou shalt be a blessing: And I will bless them that bless thee, and curse him that curseth thee: and in thee shall all families of the earth be blessed. So, Abram departed, as the Lord had spoken unto him; and Lot went with him.

Right there, we see Abram obeying God, but Lot goes with him. I question this because if God told you, then why would you take others with you? God told you and you are to obey God. And the sarcastic statement is made when I didn't take anyone with me. They went on their own. But not so. In this day and time, it is the secret meetings, the negative words spoken, the open negative actions, and finally the actions displayed.

It is evident that when a person disunites, they don't go alone they take or are responsible whether directly or indirectly for others making decisions that were not totally thought through. Now I am a strong believer that when God tells you something you must obey but God told you. God wants you to obey HIM. Satan wants you to obey him. Therefore, Satan brings confusion, disloyalty, division and separation. Did you notice what God said?

God told Abram to get out of thy country and from thy kindred and from thy father's house. Notice the order that God gives to Abram. When God tells you something to do, you must obey God. If God told you, then God told you and you must obey what God said. Obey the order of God. If you see disorder after your obeying God's order, it is your duty to set in order the order of God. If we see a brother or a sister going astray, we are to help them to get back on track. There is so much confusion going on, and we know that it is not the will of God.

And now I'm met with others that have decided to detach themselves from the local assembly because of what they now think and see. They don't all go at once. They stage their departure. Wow! Help me, Jesus! Persons that have been with the ministry a number of years, watching them grow and depositing into them the ways of the Lord now leaving with the domino effect. I do remember that before all this took place, there was something of spiritual discernment that happened in me to notify me that something was going to take place.

I remember standing by a window in my home and almost losing my strength, but I called on Jesus and pleaded HIS BLOOD, and I begin to be revived, coming back up again. I remember a zigzag over my heart and my stomach area. But each time, God delivered me. I am a strong believer in the POWER of GOD and the PRESENCE of the HOLY SPIRIT, so these attacks were very real, and the POWER of GOD was just as real and even more so. For those who came and requested to leave, they were given their release.

For you cannot hold on to something or someone who wants to be detached. Let them go. Let it go, and if it's the Lord's will if they are to be with you no matter what in time. Time will heal the entire situation as God would have it.

And then there were some that never came because they really honestly didn't know why they were leaving. They're just leaving because they see others leaving.

Many are going to give an account for these souls that they led wrong. But a charge I have to keep and A God to Glorify. I tried to convince them to reassess the situation, but that doesn't work when a person's mind is made up of nothing, or no one can convince them of anything. But time and life have a way of teaching the unteachable.

I began to take heart and believe that all was not lost that was taught and trained to them that what they receive of God was special and of greater greatness, and at some point, the fruit will come up. Hurt, disappointed, feeling unloved and unwanted, I began to release everyone through prayer. People scattered, looking for another place to worship when they had a place of worship —seeking a building, and not the true church. They did not take the time to try to work through their attitudes, dispositions, and characters that needed to be worked on. You see, the hard work of these persons' lives had been worked on through this venue, and of course, you think and feel that since the deliverance came through this way that they would be a greater blessing.

But not so. I later accepted the fact that the Lord bless me to enlist, to train and I was supposed to send yet these went. No matter where they are and with whom they are with they will still have to work through the points of life that needed to be addressed.

The Holy Writ says let a man so examine himself, and I am sure at some point I had something to do with this, but all it took was a strong coming together, working with the issues that needed to be addressed, and making the necessary adjustments that needed to be made. Left with the remnant, questions came to my mind, such as, what do we do? How do we do it? But this is the place where the effects of what have happened are truly realized and revealed. I spoke to my leader about the situation and said frankly I don't know what happened.

One thing I do know love was not exemplified.

But believe it or not, this is the place where I see God more. I begin to focus on the remnant. Loving on them, the more, and moving forward in a more positive manner with what we have and with those that are with us. Progress started happening because now I have believers.

Believers with believers. Stay focus and love more on the ones you're with. Do your best to move forward and progress. Success is still yours. Your future is still bright. In fact, it's brighter. Keep your head on and your mind and thoughts right. Forgive them, for they know not what they do.

Nothing has changed regarding your future. Your future is still bright, healthy, prosperous, and successful. The only real thing that has changed is some of the individuals with who you thought you were going to share your future are not the ones at this time that will be with you going to the next height in God or the next dimension. These are the ones the remnant plus something new and some new ones are coming into your LIFE.

Chapter 5

Life

What happened?

I'll tell you what happened. Life is what happened. A crossroad came; a fork in the road. It is time to make a conscious decision. It is time to step up to the plate. It is time to be promoted. It is time to be elevated. Life has a way of changing things. It is time to make a change. It is time for God to show up and show off, showing HIS ability to move you to the next level in HIM and in life.

Life's issues came to the forefront and batted a home run. Now you've really got issues to deal with a pure tee mess. There was a point in your life, when you were able to cope with the issues of life and they didn't bother you, neither did they phase you.

You had reached a point where you could handle that, but this is different. At a point in life, you were able to cope with the issues of others and yourself. You were able to help them through, and certainly, you had no problem dealing with the things you needed to address. But this is problematic, and it will weaken you before it strengthens, you for HIS STRENGTH is made perfect in your weakness. Are you getting this?

HE wants to strengthen you more, and this is the way that has been designed to bring this forth in you. And you will begin to speak and say, "I can do all things through CHRIST which strengthens me." Philippians, 4:13

Weaving and bowing; bending and kneeling; crying and cheering, for now, your issues of life have been magnified. Why? Oh, why? You ask. Well, now it is time to develop more CHRIST LIKE CHARACTER in you.

CHARACTER DEVELOPMENT on your part so that you can go to the next level of and in CHRIST. Remember, it is time. It is time for more FAITH. Yes, you have FAITH but not enough for this. Now you need more. You need more FAITH for this, and this FAITH will bring you the greatness that you've never seen before or experienced before. You need a GREATER ANOINTING. Yes, you are anointed but not enough for what you are going to be doing in the future. You need more ANOINTING. This is a HIGHER plateau. Let's see if we can get this in you.

Say, "I need more strength. I need more anointing." Why do you need more Strength? Why do you need more Anointing? The answer is because now you are going into a NEW DIMENSION of LIFE. A NEW DEPTH of LIFE. NEW PEOPLE. A NEW PLACE in HIM. A NEW POSITION. And for this, you need MORE.

So here comes the road, the fork in the road. The paths you must now choose to make it happen. You are going to need MORE GRACE now in Jesus Name, AMEN!

Get Ready for the Test, the trial, the Challenge, and I say the test because it takes one test with a ripple effect. I say a ripple effect. And this is the way everything occurred. One by one, or should I say one at a time, they begin to walk away.

Remember, the attack was in July, now is the ripple effect of the attacks. Remember the prophetic word that was spoken. The attack was in July, now is the ripple effect of the attack. The test… the trial… the challenge was in July now the ripple effect of the test, the trial, the challenge. They begin to walk away. When you go through some trying times in life, there are going to be persons in your life that are going to walk away.

Looking in the book of St. John 6th Chapter verses 63-71, it says, "It is the Spirit that quickeneth; the flesh profiteth nothing: the words that I speak unto you, they are SPIRIT, and they are LIFE. But there are some of you that do not believe. For Jesus knew from the beginning who they were that believed not, and who should betray HIM.

And HE said, "Therefore said, I unto you, that no man can come unto me, except it were given unto him of my Father." From that time, many of HIS disciples went back and walked no more with HIM. Then said Jesus unto the twelve, Will ye also go away? Then Simon Peter answered HIM, Lord, to whom shall we go? thou hast the words of eternal life. And we believe and are sure that thou art that CHRIST, the Son of the LIVING GOD. Jesus answered them, "Have not I chosen you twelve, and one of you is a devil?"

HE spoke of Judas Iscariot the son of Simon: "for he it was that should betray HIM, being one of the twelve."

As a leader of Christ and for Christ, we are to teach and preach and example Christ as much as possible at all times. For in Christ, there is HIS Spirit, and HIS Spirit gives LIFE. The words of Christ are Spirit. The words of Christ are Life. But there are persons who do not want to believe the words of Christ. They would prefer believing the words of man over the words of Christ. Therefore, we as leaders then have confusion because we're teaching and preaching Christ while others are teaching and preaching man.

However, we as leaders are really honestly not taken by surprise because of the inkling, the prophetic word, and the watchful eye. Keep in mind someone is going to betray you. Keep in mind that some are not going to believe the words of Christ spoken, preached, or taught. Keep in mind that some are going to leave you. This is **the Life of Christ**. And as a follower of Christ, you too will experience not to the magnitude of Christ experiences even though your experiences may be overwhelming at times, but you too will experience this walk. You will know the ones who believe not. They are not going to always believe the VISION nor in the VISION that God has given you if it takes too long according to man. But God will bring the VISION to pass.

He's just shaking the unbelievers, the doubters, the fearful, and the betrayer. You will get to know everyone and also know your betrayer. That betrayer will be revealed. It will be someone close to you, someone in the inner circle. And they will begin to walk away, and you will be left with the remnant, and yet still the betrayer will try to hang on. But don't worry, God will shake the betrayer. God will reveal the betrayer. Remember Judas St. Luke 6:13-16, "And when it was day, HE called unto HIM HIS disciples: and of them HE chose twelve, whom also HE named Apostles; Simon, (whom HE also named Peter,)and Andrew his brother, James and John, Philip and Bartholomew, Matthew and Thomas, James the son of Alphaeus, and Simon called Zelotes, And Judas the brother of James, and Judas Iscariot, which also was the traitor.

St. Matthew Chapter 26 verses 14-16, "Then one of the twelve, called Judas Iscariot, went unto the chief priests, and said unto them, what will ye give me, and I will deliver HIM unto you? And they covenanted with him for thirty pieces of silver. And from that time, he sought opportunity to betray HIM. Verses 20-25, Now when the even was come, HE sat down with the twelve. And as they did eat, HE said, Verily I say unto you, that one of you shall betray ME. And they were exceeding sorrowful, and began every one of them to say unto HIM, Lord is it I? And HE answered and said, He that dippeth his hand with ME in the dish, the same shall betray ME. The Son of man goeth as it is written of him: but woe unto that man by whom the Son of man is betrayed! It had been good for that man if he had not been born. Then Judas, which betrayed HIM, answered and said, Master, is it I? HE said unto him, thou hast said. verses 45-50, Then cometh HE to HIS disciples, and saith unto them, Sleep on now, and take your rest: behold the hour is at hand, and the Son of man is betrayed into the hands of sinners. Rise, let us be going: behold, he is at hand that doth betray ME. And while HE yet spake, lo, Judas, one of the twelve, came, and with him a great multitude with swords and staves, from the chief priests and elders of the people. Now he that betrayed HIM gave them a sign, saying, Whomsoever I shall kiss, that same is HE: hold HIM fast. And into forthwith he came to Jesus, and said, Hail, master; and kissed HIM. And Jesus said unto him, Friend, wherefore art thou come? Then came they, and laid hands on Jesus, and took HIM.

Wow!!! Do you see this pattern? Judas Iscariot was one of the twelve Apostles. He was one of the leaders. Get this picture so that when life hits you in this manner, you won't be jarred or disturbed. He conspired with other leaders to betray his leader for money. He didn't stop until he found a way whereby, he would be able to let them know Jesus identity. So, every opportunity that he got to reveal Jesus, he did, however this way, the way of the kiss was the best way.

However, Jesus knew who would betray HIM, and HE spoke it to Judas Iscariot. And it is so ironic that when Judas did his act of kissing that Jesus called him friend. Wow!!! Oh WOW!!! What does this tell you?

This says that your betrayer was once a leader, a confidant, and supposedly a friend. Be Aware!!! Pay Attention and by all means, watch the kiss.

I now begin to muscle up some more strength by praying more, meditating in God's Word more, and watching whose really with us. Every time I was given a chance to speak TRUTH, TRUTH was all I spoke. Oh yes, I told the TRUTH before, but sometimes I would be reluctant to speak or say anything because of the person/s or the outcome that might come forth, so I would hold my statements of the thoughts that came to mind. Therefore, I withheld it. I am not sure if this was quite right, but I was very cautious about speaking it and would just pray.

But now I'm more COURAGEOUS and BOLDER to speak the TRUTH whether it's to the younger or to the older. Speak the TRUTH. But speak the truth in LOVE. Speak the truth to help, not to hurt or to harm because the TRUTH will make you free.

Now when you speak the truth, some persons will get upset with you but speak it anyway because the truth is something that the devil

Satan cannot speak. So, speak it, keep speaking it, and be ready to embrace whatever comes because truth organizes, truth structures, truth delivers, truth establishes, truth purifies, and truth sanctifies. You've not experienced anything until you tell the truth.

Now you are pulling out all stops on the enemy because Satan is a liar. He cannot tell the TRUTH, and those who cannot tell the truth are under his authority. St. John chapter 8 verse 44 says, Ye are of your father, the devil, and the lusts of your father ye will do. He was a murderer from the beginning, and abode not in the truth, because there is no truth in him. When he speaketh a lie, he speaketh of his own: for he is a liar, and the father of it.

Persons are walking away, some with no notification, others with verbal indication, and others with just physical notification. Watching so-called friends, acquaintances, and families that have walked away, watching their actions and behaviors, I now say I must focus more on my assignment in the earth realm. I must focus more on GOD, and I must focus more on those who are yet here.

The question is, what was I sent to this world for? What am I to do in this world while being here for the Glory of God? So now I press on. I say press because that's exactly what it was. It was a press. Philippians 4 verse 13 says, "I press toward the mark for the prize of the high calling of God in Christ Jesus". Have you ever experienced people who do things intentionally to hurt, harm or spite you? Well, Oops that's another challenge. When all of this took place there were areas of life that were hit badly. Such as finance and income. These areas are key for survival.

But remember, when these atmospheres are present, Satan is lurking and has struck. Remember, Satan comes to steal, kill, and destroy. Jesus came that you might have LIFE and that more abundantly. Because these areas have been attacked, I now have to make some adjustments. I must now manage *finances* at this level. You say what level? Just keep reading, and soon you will know and see.

Proceeding forward, knowing that a day of reckoning will take place. Oops, another challenge. My *residence*. I now am faced with not knowing where I am going to stay or what I am going to do.

Oh yes, you better believe that I am trusting God and trying to meet everything as best as possible with what I have been given and what I have. I had a little nest that I had placed alongside for when I became of age (smile)

I would at least have something to, as they say, fall back on. But now I am in the situation that I now have to even use that. Wow! because of the pressing situation at hand, it became difficult for me to keep current with my rent. I'm now behind in my rent, trying to play catchup. I tried to reason with those in authority namely my landlord, the courts, and the attorney at large. I tried to reason with my landlord to tell them if we go this way, they would not like the outcome so let's work together to resolve this situation that I am presently in.

Let's try to work through it together. But they would not listen to reason. I am now summoned to court. The first notification I could not address because I had to officiate a funeral service for one of the parishioners of the church. You say you are a Pastor? Yes, I am a Pastor experiencing these experiences and moving in integrity as much as possible with what I have been given.

Because I did not make the first court appearance, I was summons again, this time with no alternative. Reluctantly, I went to do the right thing by my landlord, the right thing by the court, and the right thing for myself. The court, the lawyer, the judge, the arbitrator gave me until December 2007 to get my things and a new place of residence. The lawyer asked did I understand why I was there, and the arbitrator and the judge asked the same thing.

Even though God had provided some back rent and I offered to my landlord this $3100, giving them on the first of August $1600. and they received it and then offering to them on the 15th of August $1500 of which they did not receive. They decided they would not take the $1500 and that I could not afford the premise any longer, so they wanted me to leave to give it up.

Are you watching this unfold? The attack was in July, and in August, my residence effected, and persons walk away. September, I was summon to court. After going to court, I am given a stipulation that I tried to meet but could not meet. The judge and the court system said I did not have to pay any more rent as long as I agreed.

I agreed because of my present financial situation. How could I pay for rent?

And now I have to find a place to stay. I'm given three months to find a place to stay. Now don't forget the attack took place in July and these are the effects of the attack. Remember, people began to leave in August, and in September, my residence, a summon to court, and now given three months to find a place to stay.

So, I begin to pack and prepare for the move, not knowing which way I am going to go, but I must do things right, and I must go right because throughout this whole experience, I must have God on my side. I must ask God to send the Angels of God before me, the Captain of the Army to fight for me, and the Angel of the Lord to be with me to make easy and successful my way. Because "there is nobody like Jesus HE supersedes everything and everybody. I haven't found anybody just like Jesus that's why I give HIM all the praise and all the GLORY and all the HONOR."

While packing, there were some persons who I thought came to help, but I am not sure. Did they come to help, or did they come to receive information to converse about? To go and tell others for whatever satisfaction that brought. It sounds evil and wicked to me. Oh, yes, there are evildoers and evil workers, wicked folk who never want to see you progress or go forward. This is very sad. Persons who don't know how to push someone else into their place of success, operate in selfishness. Not knowing that when they push another person into their place of success someone will push them into their place of success. It is people helping people. No matter where you are now, you did not get there by yourself. Someone somewhere pushed you and helped you to achieve, and that is what each and every one of us are supposed to be doing, with and for each other.

But get this, the person who helped you and the person you helped are all connected to the next person who is pushed to success because if it had not been for that person pushing, you would not be able to push someone else.

So, see how HE made it? It is a law. A principle. A standard for success. Remember the poem? If you get this, you'll always be blessed.

There are persons who seem like they're with you when in all actuality they are far from that. People are with you when it's good, but don't let it get too rough, otherwise, they are gone. Anyway, at that point and time in my life, I just needed to see for myself who was who. So, I would receive help with a watchful eye and keen listening ears.

There will come a time in your life when God will reveal to you who really is who. At that time, don't act as though you don't understand because you really do. Jesus is revealing to you the information that was concealed but now is being revealed.

So, from September to December, I packed to leave, not knowing where I was going, just knowing that God said HE would never leave me nor forsake me. Are you feeling this? If you are feeling this now, can you imagine what I was experiencing? It's heavy, but I must go on. I must keep working. I must keep going forward, and I must stay focused, knowing that God will be with me every step of the way. I must travel this road to SUCCESS.

You say this doesn't look or feel like success. Just keep reading and watching for God is certainly revealing. You can imagine my Thanksgiving and Christmas that year, 2007. I tried to celebrate as much as possible with things packed. Thinking that I have at least a little handle on things. OOPS, another challenge. ***The ministry*** is now challenged. The place we were renting, we no longer could remain. In the meantime, the enemy still isn't satisfied, still hasn't seemingly got his satisfaction. I received a cell phone call that as of the last Sunday in December 2007, we could no longer worship where we were worshiping. Lord have mercy, I flew the roof after our church giving thousands of dollars, plus this is the way we are treated.

I received a voicemail, and mind you, it was even placed on the internet, and persons were spoken to regarding the open time even before we received a voicemail. The call was made on Tuesday, but God did not allow me to receive it for whatever reason until Thursday. God has a way of protecting HIS people even in the trying times of satanic attacks. Mind you, that in the 26 months of renting, we were late a few times, but to me, that was not a reason to handle the situation in that manner. And to give us two more Sundays that says nothing.

To me, this is a bit low unwarranted, but this is what we had to accept. After all of the blessings that God blessed us with and we were able to be a blessing. That's the final word. Lord, help us. We were without a place to worship. I immediately moved forward to secure a place for us to continue to worship, and God opened a door. This door was not as we normally would have wanted, but it was a door of entrance for worship, and for that, we thanked God.

In order to keep the remaining congregation together and to proceed forward, I did as best as possible the right thing and secured the place of worship. This was a little haven, but it was at least a place of refuge and worship. Believing that we had at least solved this problem, we continued the work.

Now the time for me to leave my residence had arrived. It is December, and I still have no place to go. Are you getting this?

Believing that I am moving toward what I believe is a great move of God, I begin on my journey. I want you to always, no matter what, keep in mind that your thought passage is essential for your survival. Even though people are looking at you in a funny way and treating you with a standoff atmosphere, you must still keep your focus on God's ability to move on your behalf.

So, I begin as much as possible with what I have to pay as many bills as I possibly can. So that as I move forward to my new place, I will not carry any heavy weights with me. For HIS yoke is easy and HIS burden is light. St. Matthew 11:30

Traveling this journey, I must stay focused, keep doing my present occupation with more dedication, be flexible, have a good friend, and be able to talk to some family members about what I am experiencing. That way, I will not have things to fester in me or to be bottled up to the point that I explode on overload. As I share my experiences with someone close, near, or in reach, a confidant, I can remain sober, sane, and intelligent.

Are you getting this.? Please do since I had to leave. My focus is changed. There is no point in trying to reason with my landlord anymore. My focus now is on something new, something better, and something of my own.

Not rented but ownership. You need to know when to change your focus. As all of this saga begin to unfold, those who looked like or even acted like that they were with me at that point are now faced with the mind challenges of thought. Such as, what is this? What is going on? What is happening? Is this God? What should we do? How should we react? But they should be praying, fasting, trusting God more, and trusting their leader would have been a great place to at least start.

Instead, they chose secret meetings, sly innuendos, and standoff atmospheres. Are you getting this? This is crazy. You've been with these persons leading and guiding as God would have it HIS ways, HIS plans, HIS purposes for 20 years or so, and now because of Satan's attack, they can't seemingly understand the present moment.

Wow! So, I call a meeting for the truth to be known and to make all hearts and minds clear of anything that is not of God. Of course, the enemy did not want the truth to be told. But remember, truth is what makes you free. It is your best weapon against Satan because Satan is a liar. Now I called a meeting. Not an arena. In this day and time, there are a lot of people that like arenas. The fight is not with man. Therefore, you must let God's way of fighting come forth.

Some persons became insubordinate, but at this point, I now have to forgive. People who think they can speak to you in any kind of way and cause more division by their words, their nonparticipation and their actions. Oh God, in Jesus Name, hold me because I know you are developing **Christ-Like Character** in me, Jesus!!! Forgiveness must be a part of you continuously. Because people really, most of the time, have no clue really of what they are even talking about. Gossipers. Whisperers.

But I must go on. I must have the thought, the tenacity, and the persistence to move forward in spite of. I must move forward. We must move forward. Remember the stories. I must go forward. We must move on. God has a purpose. God has a plan for all this. HIS will must be done.

Your life is also an open book. You have to know that as a leader, you will be faced with challenges that are mind-boggling. At the beginning of this saga, the enemy targeted the leader and then the ministry and other areas of attachment. But many are the afflictions of the righteous: but the Lord delivereth him out of them all. Psalms 34: 19

So, even though I am moving to my new residence, I must go through the process. Not knowing where I was going, I called the movers because I had to be out by a certain day and time. I called the moving company to secure their services, and the first time they came to move me, they were so confused themselves they left without moving me. Well, that's good because I had no place to go. So, praise God Hallelujah a little more time to find a place to stay.

But now I am faced with going to my landlord and asking for a little more time because the movers had some issues that needed to be addressed. And before you say or think the wrong thing, the bill was paid in advance. God had paid the bill. So, I go to my landlord to let them know that the movers had issues that they needed to address even though I complied with everything the court asked and if they could please allow me more time because I really had no place to go. I was then given more time. At this point and in all directions, you can see ***the favor of God*** from the movers and from my landlord.

Now this is in the month of December 2007.

Chapter 6

Homeless

It's a New Year. Thank you, Jesus we made it through. It's 2008 January. Hallelujah. A New year, expecting new things everything would be better. The old was gone and the new coming in yippee!!! Hallelujah!!!

Oh, no. Oops. Remember I was given notification that I was to leave my residence in December 2007, and of course, the movers came but were confused? We rescheduled another day. You say, well, "Why didn't you end the year with this being done?" My answer is, I was waiting on Jesus, and now I know Jesus was waiting on me. You say for what?

To elevate my faith in HIS capacity to work on my behalf even more. You see, it's according to your FAITH, so be it unto you. And yes, I do have FAITH but when God wants more FAITH developed in you, you will experience greater challenges in your life. However, the day of reckoning was approaching, and there was no turning back. I had to go forward. I had to move, and that was that. I then continue to order my move as best as possible, went to the nth degree day, and then did the best thing possible. I threw out some things. Things that were of no more value anymore. I gave some things away. Things that I had plenty of. I gave my landlord some valuable possessions that would enhance the apartment for the next occupant. I then placed my remaining possessions and things of continued desire in storage after organizing them.

WOW!!! I stayed as long as I could without any confrontation of shame. I allowed my landlord to view the premises before I left so that they could see the value of the vacant premises without any abuse to their property. You must remember I am a child of the KING. A servant of the Most High King and a light of the world and the salt of the earth. I must exemplify Christ at all times.

You say it doesn't look like it. And I say yes, it does for who would have thought that this was going on in my life except you were in the inner circle or a part in some way. Because whenever asked, "How are things?" My answer is, "It is good" or "it's okay" or "it's alright." Why? Because no matter what, I'd use these words to catch up to me rather than some negative statement.

You see, some persons are always looking for sympathy. But it is better to receive empathy, for there was never an indication given that God was not on my side or that I was experiencing this event in my life. If it had not been for the Lord on my side, where would I be? What would have happened to me? Where would I be? And while and after reading this, you will know that the Lord was on my side, and I am on the Lord's side. That's why I don't believe that people have to look like what they are going through.

Life has a way of challenging you to propel you to greater heights of living, and if you do not address them in the way that you should you will be forever in the state that you are in. So, let's get this move on and go on to what God has for me and what God has for you. **For what God has for me it is for me, and what God has for you, it is for you**.

So, on January 7th, 2008, with no place to go. I packed my car with the remaining items such as clothes etc., not knowing where I was going. You see, before this, I approached persons that I had been kind to help me at this juncture of life, but for some apparent reason, they decided to say no and shut the door.

Okay, another challenge, oops. Because I have to love you anyway, knowing the TRUTH. And I have to *forgive* you. So, you are forgiven,

Grace To Do It With Dignity

and I still *love* you, but this is something you now have to learn. Lord, help me. I ventured out, not really looking to go back. With no place to go, I decided to go to *eat.* Go *have a meal. Relax* and *clear the mind* as much as possible. And *thank God HE has a way all the time of covering you and protecting you*. God had with me *two friends* that were of great help, and I offered for them to go with me to eat. So, they agreed, and we went to eat.

Yes, to eat, to allow my nerves something to munch on. These two persons that assisted me in this move from my beautiful place were a great help at this point to keep me from sorrow. We went to eat. We took our time. Where was I going? I wasn't in a rush, and why not? I had no place to go. Thank God for these brave warriors that went the distance with me in this part of the saga. We ate, we laugh as much as possible, and then it became evident that it was time for everyone to go to their residence. Time to go home.

Home? Where is that? Each one of these wonderful persons had somewhere to go to that they called home. But I had nowhere to lay my head. Lord, have mercy. This is crazy, but help me. Jesus!!! God was trying to teach me something else, but I wasn't getting it yet. You say, "What was that?" Keep reading, and you will find out.

So, I made sure of some victuals from the table to take with me so that I would not be hungry. Such as breadsticks, onion rolls etc. You know the things that you take home to continue to munch on and finish that you did not finish while at the table but unwilling to leave it because you had to pay for it, and you are not going to be wasteful. So, I have to make the best of this. I have to *make the best decision* as much as possible and by all means, make *Godly decisions* even more.

One of my friends became overwhelmed with my present situation because it was unbelievable yet a reality. So, I took that friend to their place of dwelling and the other said to me, "Where are you going and what are you going to do?" I replied, "I don't know. I am just trusting God." Then their reply was, "I am going to stick with you." Whenever you are faced with obstacles or situations that are overwhelming, God will already have positioned a friend for you to help you through your trying time. You need a friend. Not only do you need the HOLY SPIRIT, you also need a friend. A real friend. A genuine friend. Someone who really means you well. Someone who is not swayed by the negative nay Sayers and negative persons of life. People that do not want to see others live or progress or be successful. Don't let anyone fool you or make you think that you got JESUS, and that's enough. Yes, JESUS is enough, but it also helps you to have someone to just be there.

So, in spite of all life's issues and problems, I proceed to move forward. You must have a ***determination*** to proceed forward in lieu of everything that comes your way. After taking one of my assistance homes, I then proceeded forward, being led to go to a well-lit Gas Station for the night —a Food Mart. Because my car is packed to capacity with clothing and other things, I cannot leave it on the street therefore I must stay with everything until the morning, and then I can place these things in storage.

But really, I still have no place to go and have not realized the lesson yet. So, I began to rest there, but the boisterous persons now give no alternative but to leave and find another place of refuge, peace, and rest. I then go to a Pharmacy that is open all night and is also well-lit, and I rest there until the morning, sleeping in my car for the rest of the night.

Wow!!! What an experience. From that time on, it has been an adventure into a life that I never knew before. Homeless!!! No place to go. And no place to call home. Homeless!!! In the street and no place to go. Doors closed because of one's own selfish motives. Remembering my help and my support to others and now experiencing this kind of gratitude.

Wow!!! The life of a homeless person who does not want to be homeless but because of life's intruders, I have to travel this way. Man, what a blow. What a shocker, what a hit. Help me, Lord!

The life of a homeless person as viewed and experienced by me is rough mentally, physically, spiritually, socially, and financially. After having to leave my wonderful place aboard called home, I had to think about what's next.

So, I search my present personal possessions that I had on me to find to my amazement ***treasure*** a card that allowed me to know after having stayed in several hotels for events that I had gained some bonus points. Yippee! Jackpot. Out of the streets in a more comfortable setting, I called, made some reservations, and experienced a little luxury in the midst of devastation. I prayed, ate, and slept much better for about two weeks. I guess you could say this was a vacation paid for by God. I never hardly ever took a vacation, and now I am being made to take a vacation. Also, my friend, who was so overwhelmed, sought to get help for me in this way also. So, with my bonus points and different ones helping me to stay in a hotel setting until God could soften the heart of someone to allow me to aboard with them until my way got better, I was able to stay in the hotel setting almost until the end of January.

However, there was during this time some persons who I spoke to that tried to bring shame to me for my present experience. This allowed me to know that when people go through a period of life like this that there are persons who look down on them as though this could never happen to them. I am saying at this time, you never know what could happen to you. So, get off your high horse and be compassionate as our Father is. A compassionate God.

I finally found out that God was working on a family member to soften their heart so that I could go aboard with them until times got better. One of my family members gave a call and finally told me that I could come and stay with them. But I still had not gotten the picture of what God really wanted me to experience. I am already experiencing a lot that I have never ever thought that I would experience.

However, in all this saga, God was letting everyone see themselves for themselves. Whether they agree with this or not everyone, got a chance to see and picture their inadequacies. Remember, my clothes are packed in the car, backseat, and trunk packed to capacity.

Wow!!! Remember I had to stay in the street because I didn't have anywhere to stay and I could not let my car be on the street so packed. And when God allowed me to find the treasure of bonus points and to receive the blessings of some compassionate persons, I was able to alleviate at points my car so that my present situation was not noticeable.

It just appeared as though I was spending a few days' vacation. How do you like that?

After receiving the phone call from one of my family members and believing that God has had a chance to work on their heart and also knowing that my vacation was over no more bonus points, I had to make a conscious decision. So, I have to **humble** myself and accept the offer and believe that God has had a chance to really move on and in one of my family member's heart and prepare to go to my family member's place of dwelling. This place had been extended some time ago, but seemingly when everything came to the forefront, they were a little hesitant and reluctant when reality set in. I didn't understand that then, but as time unfold, I understood it better later.

However, your family knows the right thing to do, whether genuinely or not, they know. Especially if this is a turn of life and not because of the detrimental things of life's existence. I did receive some married opened doors, but I did not think that this would be a good decision because of being single, so I accepted the door of family.

But was it the right door indirectly? Wow!!! This door was very stressful. It carried a lot of drama. There were vibes that I experienced because of indirect innuendos. It made me sad and carried a lot of pain. Pain that was at least twenty years plus. Lies that had been told and were not true had to be faced and corrected with the truth. This is all good, but did I have to do this at this time?

Yes, this is one of the things that needed to be faced. You are going to have to face lies and innuendos that are not correct. Face it, look it in the face, speak the truth, and face it. You see, when you stand for what's right, you are not always going to be appreciated no matter what you did or do or who you are. But you must stand for what's right anyway. My first night to go to my family member's home was a catastrophe. They had to be to work at a certain time, and I am getting off from my duty if I am not in place by a certain time, I'm out in the cold again. And of course, you know what happened.

Geared and ready to go thinking that I have some refuge, they left because of the time and again I'm out in the cold. Now it's another night in the streets. At this point, "Lord, help me" is my prayer. Not long drawn out prayers are the kind of prayers you pray when you are inadequately situated. That's why when you have the quality time to spend with God in an adequate setting, and you do that because you never know when it will come a time that you will have to just sentence it or one word it. But the kind of prayer that you pray now is short and to the point, such as Help Lord, help me Jesus, hold me Father, or one word Heal, Cover, Deliver. And believe it or not, these prayers work. They are very powerful if your FAITH is elevated to that point. They work. If you say Jesus right now, it will work. Because this first night didn't work and I had to stay with my possessions because of the magnitude of the car, I had time to think it through.

So, when morning came this time, I decided I would put my clothes in the cleaners and in storage except for the needed things to exist. And that's what I did. I waited for the morning and placed my things in storage. While I am achieving this task, my family member called and said, "You can come now." Well, you know how I felt at this point, and you probably have an idea of what I wanted to say. But, how could I? Where was I going?

Life's situations have a way of humbling you. So, I accepted the offer and proceeded to go to my family member's dwelling, and when I get there, the first thing that my family member wants to do is divide separate the company that is helping me to survive this saga. I am fighting to survive mentally, physically, spiritually forget socially, and financially is gone. Now you know something is up and something is brewing, but you don't know what. You just know that God is going to help you through all this.

Something good is going to happen. Something good is going to take place. Something greater. Something better, but it's not going to be easy. It's going to happen, but it's going to happen with a fight. I must fight the good fight of FAITH mentally, physically, and spiritually.

Chapter 7

Perseverance

A fight to survive and a fight to possess. Two fights on my hand, but both fights are the blessing to the victory that has been held up in my life.

In St. Mark chapter 10 verse 28-30 it says," Then Peter began to say unto HIM, Lo, we have left all, and have followed thee. And Jesus answered and said, Verily I say unto you, There is no man that hath left house, or brethren, or sisters, or father, or mother, or wife, or children, or lands, for my sake, and the gospel's, But he shall receive a hundredfold *NOW* in this time, houses, and brethren, and sisters, and mothers, and children, and lands, with PERSECUTIONS; and in the world to come eternal life."

But these fights will only be won through FAITH. However, Faith without works is dead. And now, here comes the *family challenges*. Never would I have ever believed that there were members of my family that would not be able to feel or see or be compassionate toward me at this time.

This, to me, was a pure tee nightmare—a struggle to survive with my own family. But I must fight. This is the next challenge. It's not an option. I must do it. A thick atmosphere of emotion that had been developed I guess for all their lifetime or mine.

This now needed to be addressed, and here I am in the midst of my devastation bringing forth TRUTH so that this family crisis that I did not develop can be resolved. Remember that everything is gone, so for me to be able to enter my family member's home, I had to be there before a certain time in order to have entry otherwise it was stressful. In order for me to park my car, I had to be there before a certain time; otherwise, I had to sit for two to sometimes five hours to have a parking space. Stressful!! While being there, I had three close calls. One was as I was sitting in the car for some unapparent reason there was an SUV coming head-on toward my car and not letting up.

My friend and I called one name, "JESUSSSSSSS" and the SUV pass by us, and as we turn to see where the SUV went, there was no SUV in sight. GOD took over. What a MIGHTY GOD we serve. There is POWER in the NAME of JESUS. When you are experiencing things such as I experienced, you begin to see the POWER that is invested in the NAME.

Another incident was as I was sitting in the car waiting for a space to park out of nowhere there came a young male running rapidly straight across the front of my car (and his foot marks dented the hood of my car and are still there today) furiously from something or someone, and again we call the name JESUSSSSSSS. I then decided to park the car anywhere just to get out of the line of mischief and firearm.

Now, in all honesty, none of this am I use to because I always had a garage or a driveway to park my car in when I arrived home, so all this is new to me so you can imagine what I was experiencing inside, but really GOD was growing me up, and I was growing up.

One other time was the experience of going into the building where my family member stayed, and as I was taking the steps, my friend was taking the elevator. As I entered the apartment a second later, there was a blackout, and a few minutes later, gunshots and on the floor, I went and you know the name we called, "JESUSSSSSSS."

Acts 4: 12 says, "Neither is there salvation in any other: for there is none other name under heaven given among men, whereby we must be saved." No other NAME under heaven whereby men can be saved other than the NAME JESUS.

That's POWER. So, these experiences were very stressful, but they brought more courage, more boldness, and more strength. Remember that I said you need to have a real earthly friend, then please believe me through your most trying hours, God will already have a friend for you to continue your process of developing in HIM. HE already knows what you need, and HE knows what it takes to move you to the next level in HIM, so HE supplies all your needs. Let no one deceive you, you did not get where you are now in HIM by yourself. GOD will always have someone there and HE will never leave you neither will HE ever forsake you. HE will always be with you and by your side. My car became my office as well as transportation for whomever whenever there was a need.

However, after being in this vicinity for a while and not being as familiar with all lawful things, I would begin to park my car and leave it. But I suffered the repercussions of that error, I received many parking tickets, and of course, you know the rest. My car got towed for parking tickets, which had accumulated from this area, not knowing the pattern of the people or the cars. So now I have to retrieve my car because I need my car for my office, my travel and for refuge.

Jesus, please help me. Oh yes, I am responsible for these tickets, and I must do the right thing and be responsible. I go to retrieve my car, and the computer is down in the banks and everywhere. Well, pay attention. This is prophecy. I have to get there to the place before 12 noon because that will start a new day, and then additional funds will be added.

But here comes an earthly angel. Thank God for Jesus. Thank God for Angels; they are our earthly guardians. Thank God for all the Angels that HE sends on our path to help us through trying times and adverse situations. The angel steps up to the plate, and I am able to retrieve my car even though the computers are down. What a MIGHTY GOD we serve. You need an Angel, and believe it or not, if you know it or not you have Angels assigned to you. But let me make you aware that there are good angels and there are evil angels. You might say, Evil angels? Yes, evil angels, Psalms 78 verse 49 says. "He cast upon them the fierceness of his anger, wrath, and indignation, and trouble, by sending evil angels among them." So, you definitely want to summon the good angels at all times. They are waiting for you to tell them what to do. The good Angels for God are Good, and good is God. So, summon your good angels to work for you.

At the beginning of January 2008, I heard in my spirit that there would be "A Paradigm Shift."

From January 2008 to the middle of March 2008, God sustained me through people who hardly ever really attended church, but they had a heart for the servant of God. Several of their family members were members of our church, and therefore they were asked to give to be a blessing to the servant of God.

Remember, in the beginning, I talked about Abraham and Lot? In the story, God said to Abraham, "I will bless those who bless you." And of course, everyone that was a blessing during this time, I definitely blessed them and prayed for them, and their family and God blessed them tremendously. These people had helped to sustain and keep the servant of God from going under. Not that God would allow me to go under, but HE used me to be a blessing to them and by them being a blessing to me. Again, I say God always has someone somewhere to move you, sustain you, help you, increase you, and elevate you to the next place or the next level. And know that each step is bringing you closer to your VICTORY. It may not look like it, and it may not even seem like it but believe me, it is, and I am a strong witness that it is. Don't ever think or feel or even say that you made it on your own. God had someone somewhere to help you. I also thank God for the remnant that was a great help in this time of need.

By the end of March, I received in my spirit a little release from this burden. I heard in my spirit "Do Ministry," and I began to take my eyes off my circumstances and my situation, and no matter what I did, I did "MINISTRY." Whatever needs I could address for anyone and everyone, I did it. You see, a Minister is one who serves. So, wherever

I could serve and be of service, that's what I did because in my spirit, I heard, "Do Ministry." I was able to teach those who God sent my way. I became more courageous, more diligent, more faithful, more industrious, meeker, and more obedient to God. I persevered more, prayed more, studied more, even became more sincere, and yes, more temperate and more willing. I was less impartial, and I asked for more **Anointing**, for God was sending me and allowing my life to go in areas that I never really frequented. This made me more empathetic and somewhat sympathetic.

Wherever I was, I tried my best to exemplify Christ and say, "What would Jesus Do?" Because not only was I on display, but my witness of being in Christ and Christ in me and being a Christian was on display. I also to help confirm in my spirit what I heard received a telephone call from someone who didn't even know me and gave me a prophetic word.

The prophetic word was, "The Struggle is Over."

You see, from January 2008 to the middle of March, all I did was prayed, meditated, read the Bible, studied the Bible, continued to serve faithfully, examined myself, and had creative thoughts of prosperity. You say in the midst of this all, you are thinking is prosperity? I say yes. Because money answereth all things. And the things that I needed answered at this point and time required money.

Thinking I had two places of refuge, I almost became content, and said, "Okay, until God can show me and help me to move from this, I believe I can make it." And just as soon as I thought that this was a great place to set up, jealousy set in, and you know jealousy is crueler than the grave. So that one place of the places of refuge closed. And of course, you know my response, "Okay at least I have the other place of refuge even though it's more stressful I can at least settle in for a moment in this area and try to make the best of it."

Remember, I told you that my car was my Office. It was my car. It became my Office. I went to work every day and was on time. I never missed a day and never missed a beat in regard to ministry and working in the Kingdom of Christ.

Whatever I could do to assist or help anyone at any time, I did and was happy to do it because I had to do Ministry. Trying to get through all these emotional upheavals, trying to keep my heart guarded, and definitely forgiving everyone who intentionally and unintentionally tried their best to hurt and harm our Christian establishment and me as a leader. I continued to press forward. Pressing on and on, and on.

Believing, fasting and praying, and trusting in God knowing that HE who had begun a good work in me would perform HIS greater task through me. Hallelujah!!! All work was done that should have been taken care of no matter what. All assignments of our ministry were fulfilled. The position that God gave me and the assignment that God gave me was still intact therefore, I needed to be faithful to God continuously.

In May 2008, it was time to celebrate. You say celebrate? Yes, **Celebrate!** Celebrate my birthday of threescore. You mean that all this took place at the age of 60 (sixty)? Yes, and it's a milestone of greater greatness, excellence, promotion, and prosperity as never before. A new way, a new day, a new plateau, moving forward, and advancing onward toward a goal that Christ wants to be exemplified through my life and in my life. So, let's celebrate. Yes, let's celebrate no matter how it looks, and no matter how it seems, let's celebrate. Really honestly and truly, life is just beginning. I am getting ready to reap a harvest of the seeds I have sown. Praise God, Hallelujah!!! Are you getting this?

So, we celebrated my sixtieth birthday. I invited persons who I really thought loved me and cared for me. And what a celebration. We had a wonderful time. And of course, you would think that everything is much better and it's okay. That I have passed the test, and yes, I have passed this test but this storm had a multiplicity of little storms and obstacles to try to impede my joy, my happiness, and my life. But the devil is a liar!!! Greater is HE that is in me than HE that is in the world.

And now, after such great celebration, do you think that that's it? I tell you the truth, that is not it. As we prepare for the 2008 Holy Convocation, we are confronted with some persons doubting and fearing because there is only a remnant. However, we persevered forward and believed God and were a great blessing to over 170 countries through blessing ministries that we were able to **seed** into. You say you are seeding at this time?

Yes, this is the right time. You never stop seeding. As long as the earth remains, there is **seedtime and harvest**. When you wake up in the morning, and the earth still remains, continue to plant seeds. Keep seeding no matter where you are, and one day your seeds will begin to come up, and it won't stop.

You see, God just needs willing people, obedient people, and people of FAITH. And mountains will move in the Name of Jesus. I believe in helping, and that's all I have ever wanted to do is help people. Some persons have said how can you help someone and you can't help yourself. You see, that's just it. That's how you look at it because honestly and truly, you have a problem helping anyone other than yourself. You help people where you are. No matter where you are, help others. And no matter where you are others will help you. ***It's a principle***.

And now, I am still confronted with family challenges that I thought were taken care of but not really. They had been suppressed and are now coming to the forefront. I had been enlightened that some of my family members were being cruel in this time of my devastation and had even become news commentators to my hometown about my trying times, yet I kept in my mind these things and continued forward.

But now the truth comes to the forefront, and even though I've allowed the truth to be known, that still wasn't good enough, and now because I do not bow to evil, I am told that I have until September to leave. Threatened and verbally abused, it was time to move on. I didn't need it anymore. I wasn't raised in such a manner, and I am not going to perform in such a manner. You've got to know when it is time to move on.

It was all okay because, at this point, I no longer wanted to even stay. I had enough ridicule. I had received in my spirit the real picture. Some persons are glad when you go through rough times, and instead of them helping you, they will say things like, "That's good enough for her," "She thinks she is better than anybody else," "Let's see her make it out of this." Not knowing that God is allowing me to see everyone for who they are so that I am not ignorant and will act with much intelligence when HE blesses.

At this point, it is mind-boggling all that I'm experiencing, but I still continue my work and continue to move forward because I am believing that there is a blessing in all this, and I am going to receive it.

So, I had until September 1st, 2008, and then this door was closed. I do thank God, though, for those family members that stuck by me at one point or another, and I also thank God for those family members that, no matter what, allowed God to be their guide. This is nothing new every family has a little of this. It is how you handle it when it is revealed and when it comes your way. You must forgive and continue to love in spite of especially if you want the Anointing to be prevalent in your life. You can't hold anything. You must wear everything loosely. For the Anointing breaks and destroys the yoke of the enemy.

I had other family members that told me to come home. But no, I'd rather stay and face this giant, and I'm not going to run and turn around, neither am I going back. I am going forward. I'm not afraid I will fight the good fight of FAITH.

So, September 1st, 2008 comes, and I must pack and leave. You say where are you going now? I don't know. I have no idea where I am going or what I am going to do. All I really know is that I am trusting God every step of the way, and where HE leads, I will follow. I packed my car and thanked my family member for the kindness, and wished them well. I sat in my car, and my friend says to me, "Where are you going?" I responded and said, "I don't know." I start my car, and my friend said, "Well, I don't have much, but I offer you my home to stay in if you want to. I know it's not what you are used to, but you are welcome. I look, I'm quiet, and I think, You know what I am thinking?"

I think that God has placed this person in my life, for such a time as this. And even though when they came into my life it was for me to help them through their trying times, and for many years no matter what their trial was, I was there to help them consistently, and now they are here to help me.

Should I say no? This would be pride, and I can't have pride to come in. What should I say? I am not use to that environment, so what should I say, "Holy Spirit, where should I go?" You know what to say. It is an open door. You are welcome. They are thankful to you, and now they want to show back gratitude. If you will humble yourself and receive the open door that God had prepared for you over five or six years ago you will be blessed. Little did I know that this would be my training ground. Did you hear what I said?

This would be my training ground to further advance the Kingdom of God in my life and in the lives of others. Time for promotion. Time for elevation.

Chapter 8

The Training

And this is where the training begins. I am now trained in more humility, more compassion, more understanding, more patience. Thank you, Jesus, for the open door. Now, this is it. This is the place that God has been trying to get me to begin HIS better work in me the more, and I've been literally running from it. For here, I have to observe, receive knowledge, and more POWER. More Anointing.

Being in a place where I've never been before and really with people that I never embraced before. In the low-income residences of New York and I must open my heart to those I'm with. I must learn their hurts, their emotions, their problems looking and being observant yet compassionate, caring, and loving.

Yes, I was caring and loving before, but this will take me to another level of being more caring and more loving. Because quite frankly, and not that I ever thought I was, but no one is really above anything. It's just that people have different *tastes and desires*. And according to your taste and your desire, you will achieve the place of your lifestyle. And really, that's the bottom line to it all.

In all honesty, we are really the same. We love, we hate, we care, we don't care, etc. and according to the magnitude of your ***education and knowledge*** of life and how to live it will determine your outcome or your results of how your life will be displayed. Your upbringing has a lot to do with how you perceive things and life itself, for we all do one thing that is definitely common to mankind. We all sit down at one time or another. We all stand at one time or another. We all go to the restroom at one time or another. So, you see, we all really honestly and truly are the same at some point or another and need each other.

God and life had me where love was really needed, where care was really needed, and where understanding was really needed, where Christ could really be displayed. My sleeping quarter was three chairs and five pillows, and yes, this was a switch from what I was use to a beautiful, comfortable, Victorian queen-size bed.

All along in this saga, no matter where I was, I never slept in a bed except for my God-given vacation at the start of this test and trial. None of this really mattered because God had given me a roof over my head and I was not out in the streets. I had a place to lay my head and clear my mind so that thoughts of positiveness could be more prevalent. Thank God for the lessons that I was being taught. Humility. Humbleness.

And so, I made the best of it. Continuing to do ministry as instructed. I helped in whatever way I could whomever, whenever for whatever. My things were still in storage but at least I was able to get a sigh of relief. I thought on these things, whatsoever things were true, whatsoever things were honest, whatsoever things were just, whatsoever things were pure, whatsoever things were lovely, and whatsoever things were of good report. Philippians, chapter 4 verse 8

I thought about those things. And we know that all things work together for good to them that love God, to them who are the called according to **HIS PURPOSE** Romans 8th chapter 28th verse. And I am certainly called according to HIS PURPOSE. It's all good.

At first, when it started, I did not think that it was good, but as this saga unfolded and I became stronger in the midst of it, I then knew God was up to something great in my life. And then I would focus on God's greatness being revealed through my life. **Family ministry** became more prevalent. I worked with families more in understanding their problems, pains, struggles, and life's issues more. All this was leading me to the **NEW MINISTRY**, my **new residence**, a **new place of prosperity** and **new relationships**.

I received a job offer at a PUBLIC SCHOOL, and I accepted it. This helped to sustain me and keep me in the midst of learning these lessons. While experiencing these lessons of life, I had people who made fun, and rejection was quite noticeable and felt. But I walked in the midst of it with my head up and my shoulders back. Most times, people don't know what they are talking about. They just love to have a conversation whether they know the truth or not. They love to keep something going.

Three times my storage was placed on the auction list to be auctioned, but I continued to fight for my possessions and to cover material that was very important. Thank God for those persons who God sent in that time to come to my rescue. Twice my car was towed for parking tickets. But thanks be to God for those persons that God sent to my rescue for such a time as that.

You see, no matter what, God was on my side. If God is for you, who can be against you? This walk of FAITH has not been easy. Neither has it been something likable, but it has been knowledge, education, experience, and enlightenment. It has strengthened me mentally and spiritually. You say, how did you make it through all this?

I prayed, and I prayed and I prayed. I kept moving forward and onward, forward and onward, forward and onward. I would analyze a situation more strategically. I had more FAITH in God's ability. I believed that God was bringing me to a place of more deliverance, promotion, and prosperity. I knew God was on my side because there was no way I would make it through this saga unless God was with me. HE had to be, and HE was and still is. Are you there?

Chapter 9

The Victory

Ministry is my passion, and whenever I was faced with opposition or a challenge or challenges, I faced them head-on. Not running but confronting. And that is what you have to do. No matter how the enemy barks or hollers or screams, you must face your challenges the first time they appear because the second time around, it would be more devastating than the first.

Looking at I Samuel 16th chapter verse 13. We see David, who was ***anointed*** by Samuel in the midst of his brethren, and afterward, ***the Spirit of the Lord came upon David from that day forward***. Are you getting this? David was anointed and after being anointed, the Spirit of the Lord was upon David from that day forward. Are you getting this?

In Samuel 17th chapter. Now the Philistines gathered together their armies to battle and were gathered together at Shochoh, which belongeth to Judah, and pitched between Shochoh and Azekah, in Ephesdammim. Look at this, the enemy got together to fight against the Israelites to take what belonged to the Israelites. ***And this is what the enemy does in your life. The enemy gets together with other enemies to take what belongs to you.***

Grace To Do It With Dignity

And the Bible says, And Saul and the men of Israel were gathered together, and pitched by the valley of Elah, and set the battle in array against the Philistines. And the Philistines stood on a mountain on the one side, and Israel stood on a mountain on the other side: and there was a valley between them. And there went out a champion out of the camp of the Philistines, named Goliath, of Gath, whose height was six cubits and a span. And he had a helmet of brass upon his head, and he was armed with a coat of mail, and the weight of the coat was five thousand shekels of brass. And he had greaves of brass upon his legs, and a target of brass between his shoulders. And the staff of his spear was like a weaver's beam; and his spear's head weighed six hundred shekels of iron: and one bearing a shield went before him.

And he stood and cried unto the armies of Israel, and said unto them, "Why are ye come out to set your battle in array? Am not I a Philistine, and ye servants to Saul? Choose you a man for you, and let him come down to me. If he be able to fight with me and to kill me, then will we be your servants: but if I prevail against him, and kill him, then shall ye be our servants, and serve us. And the Philistine said, I defy the armies of Israel this day; give me a man, that we may fight together.

I want to stop right here before I proceed so that you can receive the blessings of the Lord upon you right now, that you may receive more confidence right now in Jesus Name Amen.

Here we see and behold that you must fight. You don't have an option of whether you should fight or not. You must fight. Yet it is important how you fight. You see, Satan never plays or fights fair, he can't but as a child of God or a person of integrity. You must fight correctly. You must not be fearful or even show fear. You must show up. You must be present. No matter how tall in height your opponent is, so what? You must be visible. Your opponent may be fully arrayed for battle, but you must also know that you are also fully arrayed for the battle. You don't take any instructions from the enemy. Keep that in mind. You listen only to know or have knowledge, but you don't take any instructions from the enemy. Let's go on. verse 11

When Saul and all Israel heard those words of the Philistine, they were dismayed and greatly afraid. Now David was the son of that Ephrathite of Bethlehem-Judah, whose name was Jesse; and he had eight sons, and the man went among men for an old man in the days of Saul. And the three eldest sons of Jesse went and followed Saul to the battle: and the names of his three sons that went to the battle were Eliab the firstborn, and the next unto him Abinadad and the third Shammah. And David was the youngest: and the three eldest followed Saul. But David went and returned from Saul to feed his father's sheep at Bethlehem.

And the Philistine drew near morning and evening and presented himself forty days. And Jesse said unto David, his son, take now for thy brethren an ephah of this parched corn, and these ten loaves, and run to the camp to thy brethren; And carry these ten cheeses unto the captain of their thousand, and look how thy brethren fare and take their pledge. Now Saul, and they, and all the men of Israel, were in the valley of Elah, fighting with the Philistines.

Never be intimidated by the enemy. Know your enemy, and don't let your enemy intimidate you. Remember." you are a chosen generation, a royal priesthood, a holy nation, a peculiar people; that you should shew forth the praises of HIM who hath called you out of darkness into HIS marvelous LIGHT: Which in time past were not a people, but are now the people of God: which had not obtained mercy, but now have obtained mercy."I Peter 2:9-10

Always be obedient to your parents, whether spiritual parents or biological parents or those who have the rule over you. verse 20

And David rose early in the morning, and left the sheep with the keeper, and took, and went, as Jesse had commanded him; and he came to the trench, as the host was going forth to the fight, and shouted for the battle. For Israel and the Philistines had put the battle in array, army against army. And David left his carriage in the hand of the keeper of the carriage, and ran into the army, and came and saluted his brethren. and as he talked with them, behold, there came up the champion, the Philistine of Gath, Goliath by name, out of the armies of the Philistines, and spake according to the same words: and David heard them. And all the men of Israel, when they saw the man, fled from him, and were sore afraid. And the men of Israel said, have ye seen this man that is come up?

Surely to defy Israel is he come up: and it shall be, that the man who killeth him, the king will enrich him with great riches, and will give him his daughter, and make his father's house free in Israel. And David spake to the men that stood by him, saying, What shall be done to the man that killeth this Philistine, and taketh away the reproach from Israel? for who is this uncircumcised Philistine, that he should defy the armies of the Living God? And the people answered him after this manner, saying, so shall it be done to the man that killeth him.

Know what army you are in. You must be in the army of the Living God in order to WIN the battle. Know the status of your enemy and speak the truth regarding your enemy. So many times, the Lord has told you to fear not, so don't fear your enemy. Never run. And get ready to receive the greater blessings that are getting ready to come forth. Not that you do it for that reason, but it comes with the territory. The battles that are won are always rewarded because it really takes FAITH to fight this giant. But know that the giant is going down, and you are going to win because you are a WINNER. verse 28

And Eliab, his eldest brother heard when he spake unto the men; and Eliab's anger was kindled against David, and he said, Why camest thou down hither? And with whom has thou left those few sheep in the wilderness? I know thy pride, and the naughtiness of thine heart; for thou art come down that thou mightest see the battle.

And David said, what have I now done? Is there not a cause? And he turned from him toward another, and spake after the same manner: and the people answered him again after the former manner. And when the words were heard which David spake, they rehearsed them before Saul: and he sent for him. And David said to Saul, let no man's heart fail because of him: thy servant will go and fight with this Philistine. And Saul said to David, thou are not able to go against this Philistine to fight with him: for thou art but a youth, and he a man of war from his youth. And David said unto Saul, Thy servant kept his father's sheep, and there came a lion, and a bear, and took a lamb out of the flock: And I went out after him and smote, and delivered it out of his mouth: and when he arose against me, I caught him by his beard, and smote him, and slew him. Thy servant slew both the lion and the bear: and this uncircumcised Philistine shall be as one of them, seeing he hath defied the armies of the living God. David, said moreover, the Lord that delivered me out of the paw of the lion, and out of the paw of the bear, He will deliver me out of the hand of this Philistine. And Saul said unto David, Go, and the Lord be with thee.

No matter how the family sees you or even gets upset with you or questions you or tries to make fun of your job or occupation or even tries to make you appear as something that you know you are not or tries to read into what you are doing to keep you from going forward; You keep moving forward, knowing what's in your heart knowing your motive of why you are willing to fight the giant with the help of God. When you know there is a positive cause for your move of fighting this giant FIGHT.

Don't look to the left. Don't look to the right just look up and see the salvation of the Lord. Begin to speak positive words of a WINNER. Be willing to FIGHT. Don't let anyone deter you from FIGHTING this giant in your life or in the lives of others who you are willing to save. Rehearse your past VICTORIES. Speak your VICTORIES openly. Appropriate this giant as one of your past VICTORIES, and it will be a piece of cake being that you succeeded in the past battles and won you will also succeed in this one and WIN because of your past experiences. Be willing to stand up for God's Living Army because when this battle is WON it will be a testimony verbally and physically, and many will be WON, to the Kingdom of Christ. Receive the positive expressions coming to you to move you forward. verse 38

And Saul armed David with his armour, and he put a helmet of brass upon his head; also, he armed him with a coat of mail. And David girded his sword upon his armour, and he assayed to go; for he had not proved. And David said unto Saul, I cannot go with these; for I have not proved them. And David put them off him. And he took his staff in his hand, and chose him five smooth stones out of the brook, and put them in a shepherd's bag which he had, even in a scrip; and his sling was in his hand: and he drew near to the Philistine.

You cannot go to battle your giant with someone else's armour. You already have armour. That's why you were able to accomplish what you have already accomplished. How did you achieve that? What was your armour? What did you use? In other words, what did you do to accomplish that? Well, that's what you are going to use to accomplish this giant also. Because you know the power of the armour you have been using, and now with the help of the Lord you will use this armour to accomplish this giant also. verse 41

And the Philistine came on and drew near unto David, and the man that bare the shield went before him. And when the Philistine looked about and saw David, he disdained him: for he was but a youth, and ruddy, and of a fair countenance. And the Philistine said unto David, Am I a dog, that thou comest to me with staves? And the Philistine cursed David by his gods.

And the Philistine said to David, come to me, and I will give thy flesh unto the fowls of the air, and to the beasts of the field. Then said David to the Philistine, thou comest to me with a sword, and with a spear, and with a shield: but **I come to thee in the name of the Lord of hosts, the God of the armies of Israel, whom thou hast defied. This day will the Lord deliver thee into mine hand, and I will smite thee; and take thine head from thee: and I will give the carcasses of the host of the Philistines this day unto the fowls of the air, and to the wild beasts of the earth; that all the earth may know that there is a God in Israel. And all this assembly shall know that the Lord saveth not with sword and spear: for the battle is the Lord's and HE will give you into our hands.**

Again, be willing to stand for the Kingdom of God no matter what and no matter who. Even when your enemy makes fun of your stature you keep moving forward advancing because greater is HE that is in you than he that is in the world. Your enemy cannot curse you. God has blessed you and since God has blessed you your enemy can not curse you no matter how hard they try they are actually cursing themselves because God blessed you. Never obey your enemy . . . I can't say that enough. Express the truth as it is and know that the VICTORY is already yours. Let your enemy know whose name you are coming in. Let your enemy know what he has done. Let your enemy know that the Lord will deliver them into your hands and what you will do. Speak with courage and strength knowing that the battle is the Lord's and the Lord will give your enemy into your hands. You say when? TODAY! RIGHT NOW, it's DONE Speak it now and it shall happen TODAY verse 48

And it came to pass, when the Philistine arose, and came and drew nigh to meet David, that David hasted, and ran toward the army to meet the Philistine. And David put his hand in his bag, and took thence a stone, and slang it, and smote the Philistine in his forehead, that the stone sunk into his forehead: and he fell upon his face to the earth. So, David prevailed over the Philistine with a sling and with a stone, and smote the Philistine, and slew him: but there was no sword in the hand of David. Therefore, David ran, and stood upon the Philistine, and took his sword, and drew it out of the sheath thereof, and slew him, and cut off his head therewith. And when the Philistines saw their champion was dead, they fled.

And now this is it. Your enemy will arise to meet you or to confront you at the same time you must also arise hastily and run to meet your enemy and use your weapon of battle in confidence by FAITH and God will do the rest and your giant will fall upon his face to the ground and what the enemy meant for evil God is going to give you VICTORY and turn everything for GOOD. You will prevail over your enemy. You will WIN because you are a WINNER. You will not fight as your enemy fights. You will fight as the Lord instructs you, and you will WIN. When your enemy is defeated and is down run, stand upon your enemy, take your enemy's weapon, and whatever was the core of the problem the giant that came to take you out, you now use your enemy's weapon to take your enemy's head off (the core) of the problem. And when all those who were with the giant your enemy sees the outcome, and it's your VICTORY, they will flee and your giant will be dead. You then have CONQUERED your giant, for you are more than a CONQUEROR through CHRIST who strengthens you. Remember David was ANOINTED in the midst of his brethren and the SPIRIT of the LORD came upon David from that day forward. The Anointing was invisible yet visible, POWER from on HIGH.

YOU WON!!!

Chapter 10

Endurance

As I continued my plight in ministry, I sought the Lord's face regarding our 2009 Holy Convocation. Working in the Public School with the youth and being there to enlightened them regarding the right way of living and being in integrity, I was able to have hands-on with them.

Music means so much to me, and as much as possible, I was able to bring the Light of Jesus into their lives along with helping them to see life clearer. God enabled me to be a blessing to that school and the faculty, along with the Community. Boy, was I excited about all this, and I knew it would take more than a year to bring the Light of Jesus into them, so I paced my time with them.

Remember they say and have always said, "Rome wasn't built in a day." Nothing is ever built in a day that has any longevity. So, pace yourself as you come out of your situation. I know you want out and right away but remember there are lessons to be learned so that you don't ever have to go this way again.

And you can tell others about your experience, and they can make their own decisions about which way they want to travel. You can lead a horse to the water, but you can't make them drink if they are thirsty long enough, they will eventually drink even if no one tells them to drink. So, I worked in the school system in the after-school program. Remember, I was serving in whatever capacity that my Father wanted me to serve and going in the opened doors that my Father had opened.

I worked for three months before I received anything of salary, but I didn't stop. I kept going believing that my Father had it all under control and in control. Every now and then, I would bring it to the attention of those in charge that it may have been an oversight but remember you are learning lessons, and you are being challenged. I would always bring forth the truth because that is what will always make you free.

So, this new experience with the youth in this way was different yet most rewarding. Because you get to see other youth in a different light than what you are used to. You get to see them with their real issues and struggles, and you are there to help them through as much as possible their trying times if they let you. So, I was able, with the help of other community persons and my staff and those other persons in ministry, to bring forth an event namely, a "Youth Explosion." It was great. It showed the talents of the youth in the school to the community and to those who attended, plus it allowed other youth to come in and participate in this great event. Boy, was I excited.

All this from the expressions on people's faces brought joy and hope to a lot of those persons who were present. This was a medicine that pulsated my veins. We were able to make people at this point and time of economic upheaval to bring happiness and joy that would be medicine to their life. Proverbs chapter 17 verse 22a says," A merry heart doeth good like a medicine." So, this was medicine. Remember, the ministry was what I was doing, no matter my situation. I did not concentrate on my situation as I sought to help others through their situation.

Christmas 2008 was better than Christmas 2007. Thank you, Jesus. The Lord blessed me to work with others to help them to have joy in this season. I was just happy that God had sustained and kept me in the midst of all this.

In 2009 January ushered in a New Year, a New Outlook on things and life itself. Thank you, Jesus, for another milestone. Each day was getting better, and I was getting closer to my *victory*. It may not have looked like it but it was happening and for that I was giving God all the praise and all the glory. Coming out with my hands lifted up. And that is how you have to look at scenarios such as this. Each day, do better than the day before. Each thought is greater than the thought before. Whatever you do, do better than you did before. Never do the same thing that you were doing unless you absolutely positively know that it is a working solution to the problem at hand. I finally received a form of payment for services rendered. Thank God. Can you see things lifting and elevating?

Yes, by all means, it's happening, maybe not as fast as I would like for it to happen but it is happening. You know the song," HE may not come when you want HIM, but HE's right on time." And that was my HOPE and my FAITH. I was trusting GOD and trusting in GOD like I never ever had before. HE was my SOURCE and is my SOURCE. Sure, HE's not here physically, but HE moves through those who willingly make themselves available and accessible to HIM. No matter what good is being done, it is GOD, the HOPE of GLORY operating through you. For GOD is GOOD, and GOOD is GOD. My first receipt of income coming again, I gave to the ministry all of it. It was the first fruits of me coming out of my dilemma. I was happy to give it.

Now the next income, I begin to give tithes, offerings, and seed. No matter what. As we prepared for our 2009 Holy Convocation, God gave me to follow this scripture. Beloved isn't that wonderful. "Beloved, I wish above all things that thou mayest prosper and be in health even as thy soul prospers." Ding Dong. Click. An idea. For the Seminar Sessions, I invited A Soul Winner and A Health Winner. These were great facilitators that matched this verse of Scripture to help the Body of Christ. You say you are in this predicament and still trying to help someone else. Yes, that's how you come out. Are you getting this?

Whatever income I received, I took and invested in the concept believing that this is the answer to my prayers for others and myself.

The deliverance from my dilemma. Jesus did it. Jesus brought, it and the Holy Spirit is manifesting it, seeking to manifest the dreams and visions of others. God manifested my dreams and my visions. I finally realized that God was bringing me into my wealthy place that HE had prepared for me. So, HE had to take me through, and I had to go through in order to come to this place of wealth. Whenever God gives a vision, HE will also give provision and this is what God was bringing me to. HIS provision for the vision HE had given. That's the bottom line to it all. However, there were things in my life that had to be addressed and revealed so that I could move forward more intelligently. So, I had to go through this. So that when HE blessed me, I would know exactly how to appropriate the Blessing and not misappropriate the Blessing.

Thank you, Jesus. Our 2009 Holy Convocation was a God sent. It was definitely FAITH in action. It was all God bringing together HIS will, HIS purpose, HIS plan, and I did not get in the way of it. Whatever took place, I watched God. I didn't try to make it happen. I followed the plan and the will of God and the outcome was phenomenal. Praise God. And it happened.

Suddenly. On the last day of the Seminar Sessions, I was promised the blessing of God. As I moved forward to bring everyone's dream to manifestation on a step-by-step path, last but not least, I turned and said something regarding my vision and dream for the kingdom of Christ and the Body of Christ. No sooner than I spoke those words out of my mouth, the answer came back and said, "Oh, you don't have to worry, Bishop Brown. Something came through for me while being here, and I am going to be a BLESSING TO YOU IN A GREAT WAY. YOU DON'T HAVE TO WORRY BEING THAT YOU WANT TO ADVANCE THE KINGDOM OF CHRIST. I AM GOING TO HELP YOU. WELL, HALLELUJAH. GLORY BE TO JESUS."

That was the beginning of this wonderful Blessing that God was sending to me all along. I am also waiting for a supernatural DIVINE BLESSING, and Lord Have Mercy Thank You, Jesus, I will be able to help the Kingdom here, there, and everywhere. I am now promised security that would bring forth a continued flow of blessings that can bless the Kingdom of Christ.

My life now and my FAITH now has been pushed to a higher level. This was in July 2009, two years after the attack. That's how long it took me to get to this **statement of faith**. The night before, a prophetic word came and said you wouldn't have to worry any longer. I'm telling you what a joy and what a relief. A **statement of faith** coming to enhance the Kingdom of Christ and to bless me and others personally. Did I have it in hand? Spiritually yes, and soon it will manifest in reality but I now hold tight to the **STATEMENT OF FAITH**. It pays to serve Jesus.

Chapter 11

A New Ministry

Finances are essential and what the enemy did was he literally attacked my finances, and I had to remember and know that God is my source and HE will always give me the resources, whatever they may be, to survive. You can make it.

You can survive, but there is one friend you must have on and at your side, and that friend is JESUS. You must have the POWER of the HOLY SPIRIT to lead and guide you as you walk this FAITH WALK.

This storm came into my life, and now I thank God it's over. It took nine years and two months for this saga to come to the pinnacle of ***VICTORY***. Boy, do I thank God, and I have a new lease on life and living for JESUS. I've never tried to impress any one, I just am who I am in HIM. I love God with all my heart, and no, I am not perfect but I do seek to please HIM and to do things as best I know how and prayerfully in line with righteousness. I know, we are robed and clothed in HIS righteousness. It's no goodness of my own, but it's all HIS goodness and HIS kindness. Thank you, JESUS. Amen!

Thank God for more than enough with some to share and care for others and be responsible even more. I now have some knowledge of a homeless person's situation, and I have implemented this type of ministry into the vision of our church and ministry as a HOMELESS MINISTRY. It is so needed. Just by my experiences and lessons alone, I learned so much and am able to now use this knowledge to help someone who is in or about to go in this type of situation. Out of this, I have developed a new love for people, for ministry, and for myself. Out of this I have some knowledge of a person who is rejected, left, and abandoned, knowing that God is there and HE will never leave you and never forsake you.

Now understand I could have never gone through this as I did if God had not ANOINTED me for this test and this challenge. Thank God for the ANOINTING of the LORD JESUS CHRIST.

Also, this was developed a deeper relationship with Christ to conforming more to be like HIM. And in all this, HE never stopped loving me. Thank you, JESUS.

Chapter 12

Some Important How-To's:

1. Never look like what you are going through
You are not seeking sympathy

2. Be faithful to your obligations as much as possible
Continue to pay your bills and be responsible as much as possible
Pay where you are
Use money wisely

3. Be acceptable to people of FAITH who have traveled an even greater road of opposition and or struggle than the one you are traveling

4. Stay Prayerful
Seek the Wisdom
Get the Knowledge
Reap the Blessings

5. Have Quiet Times
Listen to hear the Voice of God
Follow the Right Instructions
Know the Heart of God regarding what you are Experiencing

6. Talk to the Holy Spirit
Everyday
All along the Way
As Often as You Can

7. Keep the line of Communication Open Always
With True Family
With Real Friends

8. Worship... Worship... Worship
God with all your Heart
with all your Mind
with all your spirit
with all your soul

9. Wear Blue Jeans
Designer if you can
Pressed... Dry Cleaned if you can
Washed... Cleaned... you press as from the Cleaners
Remember you are going up the Hill in Blue Jeans

10. Celebrate your Birthday
Celebrate whatever you can Celebrate
Celebrate You
Celebrate Others

11. Continue to move Forward
In Business
In Ministry
In Whatever moves you Forward

12. Nothing Stops
Unless you stop it
Stop Only Negative Things
Stop Only Unproductive Things

13. Be Flexible
Be Acceptable to Change
Change that Excels You

14. In This Season
Release those persons who want to disunite themselves
Let It Go
Let Them Go
Let Go of All Negative Things in your Life

15. Search for New
Let in the New
Let in the Better
Let in the More Excellent

16. Keep Working
My Car was my Office

17. Never Give Up
Keep Working Progressively

18. Dress Casual
As Nice as Possible

19. Use Clean Public Bathrooms
If the facility is not clean, ask them to clean it. Then make use of it.
If they will not clean it, do not use it

20. Store Up for the Next Day
After a nice meal… make sure you have some for the next day
Eat what you can but save some for your next meal

21. Never Hold Your Head Down
Hold Your Head Up
Shoulders Back
Be Determined to Survive

22. Do Not Compromise
Don't Settle for Anything because of the Predicament You are in
Think Better
Think Best
Think Excellent
Think What Brings Glory to God

23. Keep A Solid Genuine Earthly Good Friend
Let no one divide the Friendship
Let nothing come between the Friendship

24. Keep Sowing
Into Ministries
Into Persons
Into Productive Things

25. Share Whatever you receive with others
Share Whatever you have with others

26. Stay Positive
Keep your thoughts Positive
Keep your mind Positive
Keep your speech Positive
Keep your ears Positive

27. Keep Places of Refuge

Grace To Do It With Dignity

28. Read the Word of God
Daily
All Along the Day
All Along the Way

29. Fast
As often as Possible

30. Laugh
Comedy as much as Possible

And you will make it!!! You will receive the **Victory in Jesus Name! Amen!!!**

31. Meet every adverse situation head on
No fear
Confronting every situation

32. Be Courageous
Proceed forward in spite of
Progressively Moving Forward
Do what's right

33. Walk the Walk of Faith
Step it out
Step by step

34. Have Quietness
Quiet times unlimited
Hush… Be Quiet for a moment
Silence to hear God's Voice and God's Heart concerning your situation
Meditate

35. Keep A Positive Attitude
Positive Thoughts

\# 36. Speak Positive Confessions
Over your Life
Over your situation

\# 37. Say What God Says
Over your life
About you

\# 38. Much Scripture Prayers
Pray what the Word says

\# 39. Much Praise to God
Scripture Praises

\#40. Much Worship
Heart Worship

\# 41. Music Continuously
Music that Ministers
Music that Heals

\# 42. A Total Self Examination
Reassess You
Hold Back Nothing

\# 43. Partner with Someone for Prayer
Not Gossip
Who does not have a Hidden Agenda?
Who has been in worst situations than even yours?

\# 44. Know that you are being Sustained by God
HE is your FATHER

45. Eat from the $1. Menus
Be selective
Eat as healthy as possible
Fast Food Recommendation
Burger King/Wendy's

46. Eat at Diners
That are reasonable $ 3.-$ 5.
Eat the condiments if healthy and have not been out

47. Eat at All you can eat
Only when the food first comes out
Not after all day

48. Tithe, tithe, and tithe
Offer, Offer, and Offer
Seed, Seed, and Seed

49. Find a Prophet
One that is not connected to anyone that you know
UN Knowledgeable about anything that concerns you
One who listens to the Voice of God
One that ministers into your life
One that keeps building your FAITH
One that is an Encourager

50. MONEY MATTERS
Save up 12 to 20 months
According to your Life style
Downsize to an acceptable Living lifestyle
Budget from previous three years as a guide
Do a Median
Now may God Bless and keep you and make HIS Face to shine upon you and give you HIS peace in such a hurting world. Blessings!!!

Love is What Counts . . .

I John 5:7-21, Beloved, *let us love one another*: for *love is of God*, and *every one that loveth is born of God and knoweth God*. He that loveth not knoweth not God; *for God is love*. In this was manifested *the love of God toward us*, because that *God sent HIS only begotten Son into the world*, that *we might live through HIM*. *Herein is love*, not that we loved God, but that *HE loved us,* and *sent HIS Son to be the propitiation for our sins*. Beloved, if *God so loved us*, *we ought also to love one another*. No man hath seen God at any time. *If we love one another, God dwelleth in us*, *and HIS love is perfected in us*. Hereby *know we that we dwell in HIM*, and *HE in us*, because *HE hath given us of HIS Spirit*. And we have seen and do testify that *the Father sent the Son to be the Savior of the world. Whosoever shall confess that Jesus is The Son of God, God dwelleth in him, and he in God.* And *we have known and believed the love that God hath to us. God is love; and he that dwelleth in love dwelleth in God, and God in him. Herein is our love made perfect*, that we may have boldness in the day of judgment: because *as HE is, so are we in this world. There is no fear in love; but perfect love casteth out fear: because fear hath torment. He that feareth is not made perfect in love. We love HIM, because HE first loved us. If a man says, I love God, and hateth his brother, he is a liar: for he that loveth not his brother whom he hath seen, how can he love God whom he hath not seen? And this commandment have we from HIM, that he who loveth God love his brother also.*

Love that Counts . . .

Deuteronomy 6: 5
And thou shalt love the Lord thy God with all thine heart, and with all thy soul, and with all thy might.

Psalms 18: 1
I will love Thee, O Lord, my strength.

Psalms 69: 36b
and they that love HIS Name (JESUS) shall dwell therein.

Psalms 97: 10
Ye that love the Lord, hate evil: HE preserveth the souls of HIS saints; HE delivereth them out of the hand of the wicked.

Psalms 122: 6
Pray for the peace of Jerusalem: they shall prosper that love thee.

Proverbs 8: 17
I love them that love ME; and those that seek ME early shall find ME.

Proverbs 10: 12
Hatred stirreth up strifes: but love covereth all sins.

Proverbs 17: 17
A friend loveth at all times, and a brother is born for adversity.

Song of Solomon 2: 4
HE brought me to the banqueting house, and HIS banner over me was LOVE

Song of Solomon 8: 6a
Set me as a seal upon thine heart, as a seal upon thine arm: for LOVE is strong as death

Jeremiah 31: 3
The Lord hath appeared of old unto me, saying, Yea, I have loved thee with an everlasting love: therefore, with lovingkindness have I drawn thee.
Hosea 11: 4a
I drew them with cords of a man, with bands of LOVE
Hosea 14: 4
I will heal their backsliding; I will LOVE them freely; for MINE anger is turned away from him.
Amos 5: 15
Hate the evil, and LOVE the good, and establish judgment in the gate: it may be that the Lord God of hosts will be gracious unto the remnant of Joseph.
Micah 6: 8
He hath shewed thee, O man, what is good; and what does the Lord require of thee, but to do justly, and to love mercy, and to walk humbly with thy God

Love That Really Counts:

John 3: 16
"For God so loved the world, that HE gave HIS only begotten Son, that whosoever believeth in HIM should not perish, but have Everlasting Life."

St. Matthew 22: 36-40
"Master, which is the great commandment in the law?
Jesus said unto him, thou shalt love the Lord thy God with all thy heart, and with all thy soul, and with all thy mind. This is the first and great commandment. And the second is like unto it, thou shalt love thy neighbor as thyself. On these two commandments hang all the law and the prophets."

I Corinthians 13: 1-13
"Though I speak with the tongues of men and of angels and have not charity (LOVE), I am become as sounding brass, or a tinkling cymbal. And though I have the gift of prophecy, and understand all mysteries, and all knowledge: and though I have all faith, so that I could remove mountains, and have not charity (LOVE), I am nothing. And though I bestow all my goods to feed the poor, and though I give my body to be burned, and have not charity (LOVE), it profiteth me nothing. Charity (LOVE) suffereth long, and is kind; charity (LOVE) envieth not; charity (LOVE) vaunteth not itself, is not puffed up, Doth not behave itself unseemly, seeketh not her own, is not easily provoked, thinketh no evil; Rejoiceth not in iniquity but rejoiceth in the truth; Beareth all things, believeth all things, hopeth all things, endureth all things. Charity (LOVE) never faileth: but whether there be prophecies, they shall fail; whether there be tongues, they shall cease; whether there be knowledge, it shall vanish away. For we know in part, and we prophesy in part. But when that which is perfect is come, then that which is in part shall be done away. When I was a child, I spake as a child, I understood as

a child, I thought as a child: but when I became a man, I put away childish things. For now, we see through a glass, darkly; but then face to face: now I know in part: but then shall I know even as also I am known. And now abideth faith, hope, charity (LOVE), these three: but the greatest of these is charity (LOVE).

Grace To Do It With Dignity

Grace is one of the most fundamental words of Christianity. It is used on a regular basis, whether understood or not. However, the most defining of the word "grace" is "unmerited favor." The keyword in that statement is favor. Grace is unmerited favor expressed through the Love of God. The Apostle Paul ended some of his letters with "the grace of our Lord Jesus Christ be with you all." Amen.

Grace is favor. God's favor is expressed upon an individual without conditions. That's why we say, "unmerited favor." Favor one did not earn or even really deserve, yet it was granted and given by God. God did it. God gave it, and that settles it. It came from God to man without the decision of man. Hard to believe or accept because man feels that he only most time is in charge until he really finds out that God can and will do things without man's consent.

The Bible allows us to know that Jesus was full of grace and truth. That grace and truth came in and through by Jesus Christ. St. John 1:14 and St. John 1:17. We are to grow in grace. II Peter 3:18 says, "But grow in grace and in the knowledge of our Lord and Savior Jesus Christ. To HIM be glory both now and forever. Amen.

Paul was made a minister, according to the gift of the grace of God given unto him by the effectual working of God's power. Ephesians 3:7

*In Romans the 12th chapter the 6th-the 21st verses, there is listed the gifts and attributes granted to Christians by the grace of God given to us. Beginning with the 6*th *verse it says, "Having then gifts differing according to the grace that is given to us, whether prophecy, let us prophesy according to the proportion of faith; Or ministry, let us wait on our ministering: or he that teacheth, on teaching; Or he that exhorteth, on exhortation: he that giveth, let him do it with simplicity; he that ruleth, with diligence; he that sheweth mercy, with cheerfulness. Let love be without dissimulation. Abhor that which is evil; cleave to that which is good. Be kindly* *affectioned one to another with brotherly love; in honour preferring one another; Not slothful in business; fervent in spirit; serving the Lord; Rejoicing in hope; patient in tribulation; continuing instant in prayer; Distributing to the necessity of saints; given to hospitality. Bless them which persecute you: bless, and curse not. Rejoice with them that do rejoice, and weep with them that weep. Be of the same mind one toward another. Mind not high things, but condescend to men of low estate. Be not wise in your own conceits. Recompense to no man evil for evil. Provide things honest in the sight of all men. If it be possible, as much as lieth in you, live peaceably with all men.*

Dearly beloved, avenge not yourselves, but rather give place unto wrath; for it is written, Vengeance is mine; I will repay, saith the Lord. Therefore, if thine enemy hunger, feed him; if he thirsts, give him drink: for in so doing thou shalt heap coals of fire on his head. Be not overcome of evil, but overcome evil with good. Over 20 gifts are listed which also include offices of authority with all of the character traits of God.

Grace to Do It with Dignity

Everlasting consolation and good hopes come through grace. II Thessalonians 2:16

God's grace is available to supply all our needs according to HIS riches in glory by Christ Jesus and to help us to do every good work. II Corinthians 9:8 says, "And God is able to make all grace abound toward you; that ye, always having all sufficiency in all things, may abound to every good work."

Grace is brought to us at the revelation of Jesus Christ. I Peter 1:13 The only way you will receive this revelation is through a relationship with the Lord Jesus Christ. Spending quality time with HIM on a consistent basis daily. The Love of your life will give your life more abundantly. God's grace promotes abundant living. St. John 10:10

And the God of all grace who called us to HIS eternal glory by Christ Jesus after we have suffered a while will perfect, establish, strengthen, and settle us. I Peter 5:10

Keep in mind that grace reigns through righteousness to eternal life through Jesus Christ, our Lord. Romans 5:21 And that the grace of Christ is equated to the Gospel of Christ. We are to come bodly to the Throne of Grace and obtain mercy and find grace to help in the time of need. Hebrews 4:16 God's grace is intimately, constantly, and powerfully involved in all facets of salvation, including establishing HIS righteous character in those HE has chosen. The key word here is chosen. God's grace establishes HIS righteous character in a true Christian. God's plan is to develope spiritual sons out of those HE has chosen. Christians are called and are chosen to be rulers, kings and priests in God's kingdom. God's elect are chosen to be trained for leadership in HIS Kingdom. God calls HIS elect for an intensive and extensive "boot camp training" because God is training them for leadership in HIS Kingdom. Those being trained for the Highest Positions also go through the most intensive training in order to qualify for those positions.

There are many aspects of God's grace however, I want to key in on this one aspect. Proper prayer of thanksgiving and praise is one aspect of grace and is a freewill offering to God and Christ. Grace itself is a freewill gift. St. Matt 10:8. God's and Christ's grace provide for all aspects of salvation. Ephesians 2: 8-10 Grace is a freewill gift given for an unselfish righteous purpose to God and to man.

The Spanish word for grace is "gracias". Gracias means thanks. To tell God thank you in advance or to say thank you after something has been performed on your behalf is awesome. Because thank you or thanks denotes your appreciation for the deeds or services that have been performed in your life for your good, whether before or after you've received the deed or service. Thanks, and praise given to God and man are a form of grace. Hebrews 13:15

An example of grace is provision. There are three important things one should remember.

 # 1) Our speech is to be seasoned with grace . . . Colossisans 4:6# 2) We are to sing with grace in our hearts to the Lord . . . Colossians 3:16# 3) We are to abound in grace . . . II Corinthians 8:7

Grace To Do It With Dignity

God's grace is demonstrated through Blessings and trials and testings. However, a true Christian's life is a Bittersweet life with many Blessings and severe trials. God's grace encourages and empowers a true Christian to do righteous works of grace. Even though he may not want to, but grace moves him to do. II Corinthians 9: 8 says, "And God is able to make all grace abound toward you; that ye, always having all sufficiency in all things, may abound to every good work." Christ Himself was a man of sorrow and acquainted with grief, yet HE was the Son of God and God in the flesh . . . Isaiah 53:3 That's why we should be careful how we entertain strangers for you may be entertaining angels unaware.

Sometimes the blessings of grace are obvious and at other times they are extremely hard to comprehend. Sometimes the blessings of grace are received immediately and at other times they are a long time coming. But when they do come you are thankful and extremely grateful to the point that you give HIM praise and glory, honor and worship.

Grace is the reality of active communication of divine blessings by the in working of the Holy Spirit out of the fullness of HIM who is full of grace and truth. Grace is favor and or good will. And Favor carries with it blessings.

Salvation comes because of God's and Christ's grace. Titus 2:11 God's grace is an expression of HIS character and empowers Christians to develope God's character and provides for their complete salvation. Grace is an expression of God and Christ's personality and character and is demonstrated in how one thinks, how one lives, and everything one does finding favor in the eyes of God and man.

How well a Christian receives God's law along with his abilities will determine how he is rewarded in God's Kingdom. Grace always remain within the parameters of God's law. The amount of grace that a Christian will receive will directly be related to how well he *uses the grace he has already received. God expects even unconverted people to express grace and extra grace is given by God to the person who makes full use of the grace he has already received from God.*

In the New Testament, the teaching, preaching and ministering of Titus were a form of grace also.

Grace To Do It With Dignity

Proper demonstration of faith, utterance, knowledge, diligence, and love are expressions of grace. Grace is given in goods, services, and expressions of kindness, healing, casting out demons, preaching, and teaching of God's character. Grace grants forgiveness, pardons, goodwill, loving-kindness, and favor. Grace is expressing and showing Godly character. Where ever you see favor, that's grace and where ever you see grace, that's favor.

Three major examples of Grace are seen in the Old Testament. They are as follows:

 # 1) Joseph in the Book of Genesis the 41st chapter beginning at the 39th verse it says, "And Pharaoh said unto Joseph, For as much as God hath shewed thee all this, there is none so discreet and wise as thou art: Thou shalt be over my house, and according unto thy word shall all my people be ruled: only in the throne will I be greater than thou. And Pharaoh said unto Joseph, See, I have set thee over all the land of Egypt. And Pharaoh took off his ring from his hand, and put it upon Joseph's hand, and arrayed him in vestures of fine linen, and put a gold chain about his neck; And he made him to ride in the second chariot which he had; and they cried before him, bow the knee: and he made him ruler over all the land of Egypt. And Pharaoh said unto Joseph, I am Pharaoh, and without thee shall no man lift up his hand or foot in all the land of Egypt. And Pharaoh called Joseph's name Zaphnath-pa-a-neah; and he gave him to wife Ase-nath the daughter of Po-tiphe-rah priest of On. And Joseph went out over all the land of Egypt. And Joseph was thirty years old when he stood before Pharaoh king of Egypt. And Joseph went out from the presence of Pharaoh, and went throughout all the land of Egypt. (Genesis 41:39-46)

The next example is David:

#2) David in the Book of II Samuel 7: 4-16 was instructed by the Lord through the words of the Prophet Nathan. Beginning at the 4th verse it says, "And it came to pass that night, that the word of the Lord came unto Nathan, saying, Go and tell my servant David, thus saith the Lord, Shalt thou build me an house for me to dwell in? Whereas I have not dwelt in any house since the time that I brought up the children of Israel out of Egypt, even to this day, but have walked in a tent and in a tabernacle. In all the places wherein I have walked with all the children of Israel spake I a word with any of the tribes of Israel, whom I commanded to feed my people Israel, saying, why build ye not me a house of cedar? Now therefore so shall thou say unto my servant David, Thus saith the Lord of hosts, I took thee from the sheepcote, from following the sheep, to be ruler over my people, over Israel: And I was with thee whithersoever thou wentest, and have cut off all thine enemies out of thy sight, and have made thee a great name, like unto the name of the great men that are in the earth. Moreover I will appoint a place for my people Israel, and will plant them, that they may dwell in a place of their own, and move no more; neither shall the children of wickedness afflict them anymore, as beforetime, And as since the time that I commanded judges to be over my people Israel, and have caused thee to rest from all thine enemies. Also, the Lord telleth thee that he will make thee an house. And when thy days be fulfilled, and thou shall sleep with thy fathers, I will set up thy seed after thee, which shall proceed out of thy bowels, and I will establish his kingdom. He shall build an house for my name, and I will stablish the throne of his kingdom forever. I will be his father, and he shall be my son. If he commits iniquity, I will chasten him with the rod of men, and with the stripes of the children of men: But my mercy shall not depart away from him, as I took it from Saul, whom I put away before thee. And thine house and thy kingdom shall be established forever before thee: thy throne shall be established forever. According to all

these words, and according to all this vision, so did Nathan speak to David.

And last but not least Noah:

 # 3) Genesis 6:8 It says, "But Noah found grace in the eyes of the Lord" There are also many others but these are the ones I chose to mention for your inspiration.
Search the Scriptures for there are so many other examples of the favor and grace of God place upon the men and women of God.

Positive Words To Live By:

Proverbs 10th Chapter
A wise son maketh a glad father
Righteousness delivereth from death
The Lord will not suffer the soul of the righteous to famish
The hand of the diligent maketh rich
He that gathereth in summer is a wise son
Blessings are upon the head of the just
The memory of the just is blessed
The wise in heart will receive commandments
He that walketh uprightly walketh surely
The mouth of a righteous man is a well of life
LOVE covereth all sins
In the lips of him that hath understanding wisdom is found
Wise men layup knowledge
The rich man's wealth is his strong city
The labour of the righteous tendeth to life
He is in the way of life that keepeth instruction
He that refraineth his lips are wise
The tongue of the just is as choice silver
The lips of the righteous feed many
***The BLESSING of the LORD, it maketh rich,
and HE addeth no sorrow with it
A man of understanding hath wisdom
The desire of the righteous shall be granted
The righteous is an everlasting foundation
The fear of the Lord prolongeth days
The hope of the righteous shall be gladness
The way of the Lord is strength to the upright
The righteous shall never be removed
The mouth of the just bringeth forth wisdom
The lips of the righteous know what is acceptable

Grace To Do It With Dignity

The Proverbs of Solomon
The HOLY BIBLE
King James Version

Read these sayings . . .
Say these sayings . . .
Live these sayings . . .

DAILY and watch your life begin to change for the BETTER!!!!!!!

'CJPB

Some of the Information I acquired was from

Servant's News
Nov/ Dec 2002
What is the Meaning of Grace
By Lloyd Hobertz

All other Biblical Information was received from
The Holy Writ
King James
Bible

A Word of Thanks....

First, I thank God for this opportunity to share this experience and the boldness to share it with others who are in this present situation or who will experience this kind of experience. I thank HIM for blessing me with the strength to go all the way to **VICTORY**.

I thank God for Jesus and **HIS WORD,** which I hid in my heart, and it was and is ***a lamp unto my feet*** and ***a light unto my path.***

I thank God for the Holy Spirit and HIS ABILITY to move me to the next level and giving me the **POWER to OVERCOME**.

Also, I thank God for those friends who came to my rescue at different times during this trying time with ***prayers, help, support, and encouragement.***

I thank God for the remnant that was so dear to me at this time and did not think it wrong to stay with me through the thick and allow God to move us to ***the next level of ministry.***

I thank God for that ***special, special, special friend*** that said, no matter what, I am sticking with you no matter how it looks and no matter how it seems.

I thank God for ***my family*** that in whatever way they could assist me at different times as God blessed them with ***encouraging words, support,*** and some with ***no limits and no boundaries.*** I want to say to you I see an ***increase*** all around you.

I thank God *for the elders* in our family that gave me a *listening ear, wisdom, and encouragement, my dad and my aunt*.

And I thank God for every ministry and ministry person that could see the **HAND of GOD** through All this saga and were still **Christlike**.

And now I thank God for the hand that is helping to bring this book of this experience to you. What a person and what a blessing.

Are you there yet?
Where?
To Success
It's at your door!!!
It's right beside you!!!
It's in you!!!
Ooops . . . there it is . . . SUCCESS!!!
CONGRATULATIONS!!!
You're There . . .
Hallelujah

BISHOP JACQUELINE P. BROWN, Ph.D.

Born in Wilmington, North Carolina, Bishop Jacqueline P. Brown developed a unique and genuine love for God, His people, and a strong passion for music. Bishop Brown grew up in a Christian home, learning the oracles of God and accepting the inevitable call upon her life to carry out His will.

It is no secret to what God has done and is yet doing in Bishop Brown's musical profession. At the tender age of six, she first sat down at the piano to begin her lifelong career as an accomplished musician. She has been gifted with the talent of being a lyricist, composer, and recording artist. Bishop Brown, under the inspiration of the Holy Spirit, established a group called "The Jackie Brown Singers," which consists of anointed, Holy Ghost filled, talented singers who proclaim the gospel of Jesus Christ through the ministry of music. To her credit are two albums: *"Changed My Life" (1979)*, and *"I Love the Lord" (1989)* both of which speak the sentiments of her heart. God has also given her an additional 15 songs and is yet flooding her spirit more and more with psalms, hymns, and spiritual songs, which will soon be released in God's time. Amongst her many talents, Bishop Brown has extensive experience as a Radio Personality.

In 1986, during a two-week prayer meeting in Bishop's home, God gave her a greater elevation in Him, an exhilarating revelation, and a charge to lead His people – a call to Pastor. Bishop Brown obediently adhered to the divine call and established the International House of Prayer, Inc., now known as *International Christian Church, "A House of Prayer."* International is a multi-purpose Christian center for all people of all nationalities who gather together to worship our Lord and Savior, Jesus Christ. Through this ministry, many souls have been saved, healed, delivered, and set free by the power of an Almighty God.

Bishop Brown is also the Presiding Prelate of the International Christian Church Fellowship, founded in 2000. Through International Christian Church Fellowship, many Bishops, Pastors, Elders, Evangelists, and Leaders have come together in an effort to 'make us one' in the Christian faith. In January 2001, Bishop Brown was elevated by God and received her title as Bishop-Elect.

Bishop Brown has devoted a great deal of time to education, both in the spiritual and secular sense, and has received her Associate Science degree in Music from Kingsborough Community College, located in Brooklyn, New York; Bachelors and Masters Degree both in Theology, from Ephraim Moore University; Masters Degree in Psychology and a Ph.D. in Christian Counseling Psychology at Carolina University. Bishop Brown is a Certified Marriage and Christian Therapist.

Overall, Bishop Brown's life is a replica of the life of Christ, which compels people from all over the country to follow her as she follows Him. Her messages are presented in series form and are full of golden nuggets that enrich the lives of all who will take heed. Bishop Brown is a prestigious leader and an eloquent speaker. Bishop Brown is humble, sincere, steadfast, reverent, dedicated, and obedient to God and His Kingdom work. She continues to be a tireless encourager to others, and **FAITH** is the lifeline to her ministry and success.

More than anything, Bishop Jacqueline P. Brown **LOVES THE LORD!** She is saved, sanctified, Holy Ghost filled, anointed, appointed, chosen, and qualified by God to preach the awesome Word of God.

She continues to proclaim everywhere she goes, *"THERE'S NOBODY LIKE JESUS; HE SUPERCEDES EVERYTHING AND EVERYBODY. I HAVEN'T FOUND ANYBODY JUST LIKE JESUS, THAT'S WHY I GIVE HIM ALL THE PRAISE, ALL THE GLORY, AND ALL THE HONOR!"*

www.ingramcontent.com/pod-product-compliance
Lightning Source LLC
LaVergne TN
LVHW091559060526
838200LV00036B/914